My Darling Nellie Grey

My Darling Nellie Grey

George Bowering

Talonbooks

Copyright © 2010 George Bowering

Talonbooks
P.O. Box 2076, Vancouver, British Columbia, Canada V6B 3S3
www.talonbooks.com

Typeset in Minion and printed and bound in Canada.
Printed on acid-free FSC certified 10% post-consumer recycled paper.

First Printing: 2010

The publisher gratefully acknowledges the financial support of the Canada Council for the Arts; the Government of Canada through the Book Publishing Industry Development Program; and the Province of British Columbia through the British Columbia Arts Council and the Book Publishing Tax Credit for our publishing activities.

No part of this book, covered by the copyright hereon, may be reproduced or used in any form or by any means—graphic, electronic or mechanical—without prior permission of the publisher, except for excerpts in a review. Any request for photocopying of any part of this book shall be directed in writing to Access Copyright (The Canadian Copyright Licensing Agency), 1 Yonge Street, Suite 800, Toronto, Ontario, Canada M5E 1E5; tel.: (416) 868-1620; fax: (416) 868-1621.

Library and Archives Canada Cataloguing in Publication

Bowering, George, 1935–
My darling Nellie Grey / George Bowering.

Poems.
ISBN 978-0-88922-634-0

I. Title.

PS8503.O875M9 2010   C811'.54   C2009-906976-8

Thanks to the publishers of these limited edition chapbooks:

Crows in the Wind, BookThug, Toronto (Jay MillAr)
A Knot of Light, No Press, Calgary (derek beaulieu)
Eggs in There, Rubicon Press, Edmonton (Jenna Butler)
U.S. Sonnets, Pooka Press, Vancouver (Warren Dean Fulton)
Montenegro 1966, No Press, Calgary (derek beaulieu)
Some Answers, LaurelReedbooks, Mt. Pleasant (Kemeny Babineau)
Shall I Compare, Beaver Kosmos, Penticton (Cathy Miller)
According to Brueghel, Capilano University Editions, North Vancouver (Jenny Penberthy)
Fulgencio, Nomados, Vancouver (Peter & Meredith Quartermain)
Tocking Heads, above/ground press, Edmonton (rob mclennan)
Valley, No Press, Calgary (derek beaulieu)
There Then, Gorse Press, Prince George (Barry McKinnon)

An earlier version of "Prizren" was published in *In the Flesh*, McClelland & Stewart, Toronto, 1974.

Especially for Victor Coleman and Roy Kiyooka

Introduction
11

My Darling Nellie Grey

Crows in the Wind
21

A Knot of Light
55

Eggs in There
85

U.S. Sonnets
119

Montenegro 1966
151

Some Answers
185

Shall I Compare
217

According to Brueghel
251

Fulgencio
285

Tocking Heads
317

Valley
351

There Then
383

Introduction

Here it was, the last week in December of 2005. I had just experienced my seventieth birthday, but I still couldn't believe it, despite the wonderful anthology my wife and poetry friends had made for the occasion. I'd finished up some jobs that had been cluttering my desk, and needed something to distract me from the idea of having to write the memoir/novel I had suspended work on.

I wanted to say something. I wanted a new project. It struck me that a new year was going to start in a day or two, and I had never really made a New Year's resolution, ever. What if, I asked myself and no one else, what if I were to write a page of poetry every day, winding up with a 365-page poem? There aren't many of those around. Then I had an attack of the sensible(s). Okay, what if I were to write a page every day, but make a dozen poems, or maybe a dozen monthly parts of a long poem? What if, thinking ahead, I aimed at getting a chapbook published for each month, and then a 365-page book made from those twelve chapbooks of thirty, or thirty-one, or twenty-eight pages?

Oh, sure. Nothing grandiose.

No, I thought, it will be a discipline. All my life I have been pestered by people suggesting discipline.

So when January 1, 2006 came around, what could I do? I opened a notebook and wrote: "When this idea/ found a way to reach me/ it was worn." As the poem progressed, it seemed to be about someone with the habit of seeing the world through poetry, and the world this third-person figure sees includes beauty and reality, the two words whose top halves resemble each other, even while he wonders whether he is entering the old age of a wise man or a fool. That January poem fills up with another USAmerican war and whatever else comes his way, including the death of Irving Layton, the other mortality called the news, the necessity of being long in the world headed for the earth. It became another elegy, *Crows in the Wind*, and I heard it after thirty-one days, familiar music, the way I made poetry when I could do it the way I like to read.

But when it was over I said all right, there will not be another part like that; from now on each chapbook will have a challenge. Back in the day, I would write poems with formal rules or distractions I called "baffles." One, for example, would examine a crisis in love by turning over random tarot cards one at a time and responding to the images, trying to keep my mind off the poem's continuity. It worked. I told people that the other poets working this way were Victor Coleman and Roy Kiyooka. Victor, for example, wrote a long poem, *America*, which was acrostic at both ends of its lines.

Back in the day, I had not heard of the OuLiPo. The *Ouvroir de Littérature Potentielle* was formed in 1960 by novelist (and amateur mathematician) Raymond Queneau and chess master François Le Lionnais, to investigate the possibilities of applying mathematical structures to literary creations. Soon the organization grew to include twenty-nine writers and artists and mathematicians, most of them French, meeting first as a sub-committee of the *'Pataphysique* group (so much admired by bpNichol), but then striking out on their own. For nearly half a century they have been meeting with famous regularity and proposing various applications of restraint (what I had called baffles) to texts. It was not long until formal methods of composition other than mathematical were being explored.

Among the most famous examples of OuLiPo texts are Italo Calvino's *If on a Winter's Night a Traveller*, in which the reader has to make his way through chapters from detective books or Japanese erotica, etc., "accidentally" inserted in the main text, and Georges Perec's *La disparition*, a novel about something missing, composed without using the letter *e*. In the Spanish edition, it is the letter *a* that is missing because it is the most common letter in that language.

As the years have gone by, more and more Oulipian texts have become available to us, partly through the efforts of Harry Mathews, the only USAmerican member elected to the group. In Toronto in recent years several writers, including Victor Coleman, Christian Bök and André Alexis, have claimed the influence of OuLiPo. As an acolyte unaware all those years, I am proud to have been mentioned in the big *Oulipo Compendium* (London, 1998).

The first Oulipian book I ever read was Queneau's *Exercices de style* (1947). Actually, the first time I read it was in Barbara Wright's English translation, *Exercises in Style* (1958). My UBC linguistics professor Ron Baker recommended it to me in 1960. Although my poetry at the time was doggedly faithful to the notion that writing verse was a record of speaking verse, I was exhilarated by this *texte*.

Queneau wrote ninety-nine short texts that tell a trivial story over and over. On a bus he sees an altercation between two men, then later sees one of the men in lively conversation with someone else at a train station. Queneau tells that story as a narrative, as a blurb, as a telegram, etc. Wright, due to differences in the properties of languages, makes some substitutions in her U.S. edition. So does Umberto Eco in his Italian translation. There were substitutions, too, in the stage version I was fortunate to see one spring in the 1990s, wherein texts became short performance pieces by three members of the company *Théâtre à Suivre* of Toulouse.

Texts, I now understood, are not there to replicate life, but to generate something else, including further texts.

In February 2006 I wrote *A Knot of Light*, the shortest of my twelve chapbooks in the series. It would echo and elaborate passages in the January text, but the poem was generated by my wife's comic acts in the kitchen. The daily sections would consist of two stanzas of short lines highly attentive to the sounds of vowels and consonants. There would be two four-line stanzas or two five-line stanzas. The crows in the previous poem are joined in the February text by a lot of other birds, all of them vocalizing, one hopes.

It was back to thirty-one sections in March for *Eggs in There*. It is my second "I Remember" book, the first being *The Moustache*, which was about the painter Greg Curnoe. The "I

Remember" book was invented by Joe Brainard, a U.S. artist who was a friend of the Oklahoma poets who became part of the New York School. It is an easy compositional method, actually, in that you just write "I remember" to introduce a line or a paragraph or a page about the subject you have in mind. Brainard wrote a number of such works, and while they are not Oulipian by any means, the form was picked up by some writers in the group, first Georges Perec, who wrote *Je me souviens* (1978). When Perec died, his fellow Oulipians collaborated on an "I Remember" performance, and Harry Mathews wrote an "I Remember" book about his departed friend, *The Orchard* (1982). Jacques Bens, a founding member of Oulipo, even wrote an "I Forget" book.

My "I Remember" book is about my parents. That seemed the most normal thing for me to do.

Of course one of the oldest and most obvious of formal poetic constraints is the sonnet. In April I wrote thirty *U.S. Sonnets*. I put the periods after those first two letters to make sure that no one thought I was using the first person plural. These are sonnets only in that each is made of fourteen lines, in this case seven two-line stanzas with pretty long lines. They are almost found poems. Half of them are quotations from U.S. sources, from the racist Declaration of Independence, to misspelled hate slogans carried by Texas rednecks (no, not that one—he was on the cover of the chapbook), to advertisements for gun shows. The other half are descriptions of photographs offered up by U.S. daily life—advertisements for patriotic jockstraps, KKK families with their sordid outfits, etc. I don't know whether April is the cruelest month, but it can be cruelly funny, I thought.

In the world outside of poetry, May is my favourite month. In May of 1966 I went to Europe for the first time, on a Volkswagen bug ride with my friend Tony Bellette. This six-week trip occurred on the 150th anniversary of Percy Bysshe Shelley's six-week voyage on the Continent. Just in case no one else was going to do so, I thought I'd write a "travel poem" to commemorate the fortieth anniversary of mine.

During that trip I did a lot of writing. I wrote two thousand words every night on my portable typewriter, about the day's doings. This stuff I made into a travel book called (blush) *Eye Kicks in Europe*. It's in a file in Ottawa. I also wrote a letter home every night, half of them to my wife. Then I wrote every night in my diary. That's where I went for the details that show up in my May 2006 chapbook *Montenegro 1966*. But don't be surprised if you suspect references in there to the other eleven volumes in this book. You will notice that the poem ends with hail hitting the roof of the VW beside a highway in Yugoslavia. More poems could have made the move out of personal prose, but May, nice as it is, stops at thirty-one days.

For June I went to a gimmick I have used before, though usually in shorter runs. I took famous questions posed by famous poets in their famous poems, and wrote what I think is a poem made up of replies to those questions. I picked the famous poems in random order, then tried to keep some kind of story going— not a narrative, but a reluctance of certain images to get left behind, I guess. It seems to be mainly about air, what we breathe, what music we let go, what wind reminds us of the birds in the first two books in this yearbook.... It is air that we use to make poems, simply. But let's not do things simply, not all the time.

What poems strike us as simpler than the love poem sent as a kind of posy to the loved one, perhaps enumerating her charms? Remember that centuries ago good old Shakespeare sought to complicate this practice with his beautiful querulous sonnets. That's where I got my July title, of course. Then I tried to duck under Shakespeare's arm and see whether I could get that simple, to write with some airy music and lay myself bare as a courtier of the early twenty-first century.

So in order to do that I had to set up a constraint that was not complicated but which was strict. Well, when I was a kid my favourite number was three. When I was a young man it was nine. Now it is twenty-seven. So *Shall I Compare* is a love poem to Jean Baird, and it is interested in numbers. It enumerates her attractive parts, starting with her hair and heading for her toes. Each day there is a little poem made of twenty-seven words.

Each has three step-down stanzas, and each step is made of three words. $3 \times 3 \times 3 = 27$. Go thee forth and multiply, I heard the guy say. It adds up, I say, to a loving male gaze. Oh, and the lady and I got married two-thirds of the way through the writing of the poem.

My gang and I are fond of returning often to William Carlos Williams's late sequence *Pictures from Brueghel*, especially to the one that replies to Brueghel's painting that includes the legs of Icarus as he falls into the sea off the coast of Belgium. In school we had learned that W.H. Auden, too, had written about this painting, but he had used it as an *example* of something. In contrast to that, the Williams poem offers his line of thought while focusing his eyes on the picture. So his poem begins, "According to Brueghel when Icarus fell it was spring." The poem goes to the bottom of the page in short lines without graphic punctuation, a stream. There we find the little detail of legs in the landscape, something a viewer of the painting might not notice until his eyes at last go to the bottom right corner of the canvas. Williams was working with something that he or someone else called an "experiment in American measure."

I had done the odd ekphrastic poem in the past, and since we were going to go to Italy in August, I thought why not a series of "According to" poems, imitating the form found by my hero WCW? The first half of my August chapbook responds to paintings from various sources, some of them Canadian. Then when we got to Rome Michelangelo took over, to be followed by other artists encountered in the city and around Tuscany. You will notice that certain subjects show up more than once, as often happened in the Renaissance. I love Williams above other poets, and I am ravished by the Italian Renaissance. August of 2006 was a wonderful month in my eyes.

The September chapbook is not restrained in any obvious formal way, but overtly political poems have always been a part of my output, and there is a sense in which this entire year-long project is a kind of sampler, isn't there? Besides, history is itself a rather uncompromising constraint. Fulgencio Batista was normal when I was a teenager, just like all the other U.S.-sponsored dictators in Latin America. When he was chased out of Cuba (along with most of its money) I was twenty-three, getting ready for the sixties and for poetry. We young poets had him the way Shelley had the Habsburgs.

I guess that some people might see the poem I wrote about Cuba as what they used to call "anti-poetical," but one has to listen to a poem, too, and I hope that there is something, if not musical, at least sound-textured about it.

If you are used to getting your news from talking heads on television, you might not be a newspaper reader. I hear that we are getting thinner on the ground. I have always been interested in headlines and the ways they are made. When my pal Willy and I were young, I used to read the sports headlines to him. He knew nothing at all about sports, and so would feign exaggerated emotional reactions when I read, for example, "MOUNTIES STOMP ALL OVER PADRES;" even worse, "OTTAWA BOMBS ESKIMOS;" and during the hottest part of the cold war, "REDS DEMOLISH YANKS."

Unlike July, October was dreadful. Early in the month, just after we had come back from a quick trip to San Francisco, the news came that Jean's daughter Bronwyn had been killed in a car accident. If there were ever any excuse to give up on the New Year's resolution, the insane days before and after Bronwyn's funeral in small-town Ontario would have provided it. But the poem I had barely started was easy to access and continue, and maybe I even needed it to continue during that time of raw crazy grief.

The main restraint consisted of reading the newspaper every morning, and finding a headline that was misleading or at least ambiguous—to read literally what the headline maker had given little thought to. Continuity was not much of a problem, partly because some stories went on for days, and partly because headline makers fall back on their tried and true formulas. I do not remember having any trouble finding material that was funny. You can do it any day—let me just look at today's *Vancouver Sun*. Hmm: "WORLD'S TOP TEN ISLANDS OFF THE BEATEN TRACK." Reminds me of the time Jack Kerouac said, "Walking on water wasn't built in a day."

Some poets are easily associated with a place in which they live or used to live. We have the Gloucester, Massachusetts of Charles Olson and the Prince Edward County of Al Purdy. On a smaller scale, I return time and time again in stories and poems to the southern Okanagan Valley of my childhood and youth. A few years ago I was lucky enough to visit Lorine Niedecker's cottage beside the Rock River near Ft. Atkinson, Wisconsin. Her world, between the great St. Lawrence River system and the great Mississippi River system, would seem opposite to the desert valley I came from. Niedecker's first volume of collected poems was titled *My Life by Water*. How neat it was to peer through the window of her place on Blackhawk Island, to see the imperfect linoleum, to look in as she looked out on the water that also oozed through the soil under her floor.

Are you old enough to remember those little books we would get at the drugstore, a little wider than they were high, each page a different colour, their use being to gather autographs and corny remarks from our friends? Lorine Niedecker wrote a couple of poems in those books. One is called *Paeon to Place*, and Niedecker said that she wanted it to be published separately. It was written in 1969, and it was published as a facsimile edition in 2003, to honour her hundredth birthday.

Her book is filled with alliteration and other rimes, beginning (in her hand, remember) this way:

>Fish
>>fowl
>>>flood

>Water lily mud

>My life

I didn't lay it on quite so insistently, but I did want my piece to be a friend's response. An obvious constraint is the use of five "lines" per page. More important—in my first page you will hear the sounds a letter *a* might indicate. And so on. I don't expect anyone to make a long trip to see the place I came from and wrote about, but I like to imagine someone reading this November's poem out loud.

I have always liked alphabet books, and have written quite a few. I also like the alphabet itself. It is repeated in an order that we all agree to, or at least follow, but it is an order that has no extrinsic meaning. It is outside the worlds of humanism, cause-and-effect, realism, logic, and so on. If you want to give up control of your materials, go for the alphabet. Sometimes I read alphabetically, a book by Atwood followed by a book by Beckett followed by a book by Charyn, and so on. When I am in bed waiting to go to sleep I play the alphabet game in my head—ten cities that start with *A*, and so on.

So for this December text, the poems had to be written alphabetically and read alphabetically. The sounds will accumulate, and rime will find our way, and so on, but here is the rule: the title will tell us the name of a city I have lived in or at least visited, and also the year in which that happened. Then at the bottom right corner of the page three other cities are named. I could have written a page about any of them, or you can if you have been there. That is another way a text can continue, a constraint for you the reader as writer.

But where have we really been? The last word for December and for 2006, before I leave you with the names of the last three cities, will tell you.

Crows in the Wind

January

1.

When this idea
               found a way to reach me
it was worn,
         its shoulders ached, it
felt like it was dying,
              it needed
a place to stay.

          Here, where two eyes
ache with something tied to age
is an attempt to escape
the first person on the first day, to say
enough, you sit still,
               let the poor thing
rest, remember when you required love
manifested as letting be.

A crow in the wind
seems to know
as much as you do.

2.

He giveth to the beast his food,
and to the young ravens which cry.

A faint smudge of happiness
comes down the hill,
or is it a brown car
depending on its brakes?

    Thus one sows doubt
    early in the year
    that looks, at rare times,
    like his last
    or the truth at last.

What hangs in that
you'll need to know
the weather to know.

3.

He thinks the slippery trees feel pain
    when the wind whips them,
all their birds being nurses
    out of sight.

While on the treeless plains
    of Mesopotamia, U.S. warplanes
fix bombsights, fearing history,
    dreading birth of the alphabet.

He adored "America," little kid
    pisspants, not a care in the world,
(most horrific fall outside it)
    wearing Rule Britannia shirts

and scabs on both knees. Pain
    was manageable, wind
made patterns in the sand, pyramids
    filled his eager hurried brainpan,

    Cheops, great grandfather.

4.

Whether to know,
      or just abide,
to lie on your back
      these last days

is no question for
      a colonized brain.
Envy not the oppressor,
      and choose none of his ways.

Let him gobble crude,
let him invent longer needles
to pierce fat bums,
let his tanks
      rust in creekbeds,

let his carcass
      ooze oil when he sits
in his extra wide
      reclining chair.

5.

The old ravens cry now,
the broken nose poet is dead,

there might not be a heaven,
there might be dust.

                      You hear that poetry,
it caws, it caws, it is darkness
itself, shifting feathers, ungainly hopping,

a muse you can expect
        on the fence behind your house.

Gone now, you with him, you
who were in his head a moment
now never.

        Learn, while you have time,
a bird-call.

6.

The mother murmurs a quick prayer,
the children too terrified to scream
crowd her, the foreigners in shock costumes,
oily rifles in their hands,
> smash everything with huge heels,
> shout in an unknown language,
> looking for boys to kill,
> leave blood and filth behind.

They must have come from those high
aircraft, they and their anger.

> As a bird hasteth to the snare,
> and knoweth not that it is for his life,

so these disguised youth
unpin their future as ours,

end the day washing oil from their bodies.

7.

Under the lid of the earth
or in the downtown east side,
we settle for death
or life.

We spend all our days settling,
looking up occasionally at an orange banner
or into a bowl of clam chowder
red as Long Island.

Settling like earth itself,
not for less but for comfort,
to be fragments among all fragments
and hence the whole.

8.

Old crow,
inherit the wind.

It will be your estate,
winter for all time

under the wheel, then
just under.

9.

Twenty-three days of rain,
a prime number in the weather,
no change

but a brassy U.S. dollar on my desk,
a dog barking loudly behind me,
a muse gone under
the weather at least.

                    I'll live another way;
there is no virtue in poetry, no honour
in verse, only a habit
easy to break, no
stake.

10.

How soft the rain,
        how easy the street side
where no alien machines
        turn their long gun barrels.

When those monsters lost their king
they lost their peaceable kingdom,

they forgot the sweet contradictions
in the mind of their prophet,

till munitions became
        their national product;
children benumbed by wires in their ears
became suicide bombers
        at the city library.

11.

Inside those frightening outfits
are boys with ignorance,
short memories,
home-
sickness.

Rue.

The glory of young men
    is their strength:
and the B E A U T Y of old men
    is the grey head.

It remarks the difference or not
between B E A U T Y and
    R E A L I T Y

12.

Beside the freeway,
        standing water in fields
where a province fetches up,
        while above us clouds of crows
hie themselves to their famous
        mysterious rookery.

Fifty-three years ago
        it was this wet here,
but he was in the snowy mountains
        and you weren't even born.

This is the soft rain.
It will come this way again.

But he will not, you
will remember his grey head.

13.

Remember when you required love
disguised as letting be.

There is so much to let be,
even poetry to let be.

But the book not written
will be opened by a patient ghost.

And all your uncertainties
will be a wind you are trying to

tie into a bundle.

14.

Rise at noon,
and the hours speed before you.

Fall behind you
into the never again.

Suffuse your limbs
with the present life of a sloth

filling its grey head
with someone's idea of never.

15.

On the morn when we are supposed
        to tie the record for rainy days
the sky is blue, white clouds
        here and there, so I close the blinds

and dream of being a god
        who can make the weather, that god
who hath gathered the wind
        in his fists, that unfilial eye

aching and crusted, scabbed,
        incapable, that eye—
the ravens of the valley
        will pick it out

and the young eagles shall eat it.

        Carrion
        on a clear day.

16.

    To have come this far
only to spend a morning
        over a text, wondering:
have I become a wise man
        or truly, a fool?

        And, infinitely, to wonder:
which is it that
        so wonders?

17.

A fool's voice is known
  by amplitude of words.

I read page 1200
  of my morning book,
this first person of late, single
  before the multitude, I

who has laboured for the wind,
  I go,
   a lorn monster hungry
   in the imagined snowy forest.

18.

One wind for the mouse,
        another for the crow,
and do we know, do we know
        which we are?

Wise man or fool,
        do we live in the house of mirth;
do we know the weather
        here on earth?

Rain before seven,
        shine before eleven.
But then
        do we know the time?

19.

Of making books there is no end,
and you have always known
you will die with pages to go,
you will go
         out of print,
         out of fashion,
         out of mind,
into the wind.

And look, there's a young guy,
not much chin, no colours in his clothing,
sitting moony in your café,
his muscles gone west,
but a gorgeous long poem in his skull.

You could tell him,
you could impersonate a muse or sailor,
you could show him his future.
You could offer to trade.

20.

No, BEAUTY is not REALITY,
not by half, nor is it
sublime.

      You are beautiful, my love;
there are soldiers around your bed,
swords at their thighs.

You are a riddle of bones,
no mystery,
no secret flesh;

you are visible, all colours,
comely as can be.

A weak January sun shows me
your breasts are
nothing like roes,
lovely as they might be.

21.

His head is as the most fine gold,
his locks are bushy, and black as raven

in my dream of 1961, but here am I
again, eyes open, first person, he

sits beside me, thick hair white, head white,
eyes hiding some white in there somewhere.

We can see, we can speak from a stage,
we can draw humans with peculiar
wiring systems inside their skulls.

We can hope to outlive the approach
of new illness, poets
have to do that,
we have to show them how to
evaporate in the still air.

22.

A voice from the mad
on my telephone, I swim
a wind I recognize but can not name.

She was nearly my sister,
now wrack in an unknown ward,
dreaming awake where Beethoven?
      He was her grandfather's
      great uncle,
      crazy music at the end,
an absolute quartet we deserve, a test
of our power to think, a great deep
      cello
      reverberates upward through my (viscera).

It is only another way someone tells me
the rope is on fire.
      The rookery is full.

23.

    Je sens que des oiseaux sont ivres
D'être parmi l'écume inconnue et les cieux!

And I, up in a window, shod in a tired
body, fly only into my own past, a
childhood dramatized, a voice in the wings,
an insistent grasp of a pen that looks
like this one, aimed at whatever
flies past my pane of glass.

My crow's nest.

Et, peut-être, les nâts, invitant les orages
Sont-ils de ceux qu'un vent pench sur les naufrages

Perdus,

    if this was ever a ship afloat,
a boat full of drunken birds.

24.

Le noir roc courroucé que la bise le roule
    unwilling to wait for stone or bird,
black stone already in place,
    one's face
    up, one's grace
    gone, one's race
    long ago run.

That wind, we were instructed,
was an omen of change, but no,
    this time it gathers one,
    promising an end to change,
a friend to hear from never more at all.

25.

As he noticed he was occupying age,
people from his youth reached him,

his youth reached him,
he learned what had happened
to everyone. His life, as he called it,
grew to be a mansion
with many rooms lighting up.

And his heart was moved,
and the hearts of his people,
as the trees of the wood
are moved with the wind.

26.

I am a magpie after all.
I fly only to reach the good stuff.
I have been doing this all my life.
I have met many fliers along the way.
I am a black and white bird.
I become hard to find in the snow melt.
You can locate me by the loot.
You can decide not to read it.

27.

The wind
off the sound
on Water Street
in Port Townsend

can make you glad
you're alive
barely, just
barely,
alive
and in love.

28.

What, he said, is not wet
in La Connor, even
the wild turkeys, brought here
by some stray wind
have shoulders whose main purpose
is to illustrate moisture.

29.

I watched my father
      take a bar of white soap
into the lake,
          knew I was learning
another way of my people.
                We wash
in the place where we play, we
work there too, we don't
      call it "nature," it is only
what is afforded us,
             we take
a bath and what is granted
and give back what we can.

30.

He can't bear the thought
    of being ashes in an urn.
It's too small. A coffin
    is bad enough, claustro-
phobia enters his skull,
    enclosed, almost air-tight,
open to the elements,
    starting with fire.

31.

Two eyes ache
      with something close to age,
this last night of the month,
      a wind we've been warned of
driving winter's rain
      across my window black as Newlove.

Why do I half believe
      it is the world grown old
where I keep my body all these years
      out of the ditch, above the ground,
half in the sight of strangers
      I woo for a scant fame.

Today we went to a gallery
      to admire the paintings of
a dead friend,
      and they spoke to us
      as if Jack were alive, grinning
      under his soft hat.

Do we need him any less
      than we need ourselves?

A Knot of Light

February

1.

On the first
day of Feb, you
pulled my
pants down, in
the kitchen.

I'm not, you
know, bitching,
I can gather
myself together,
given time.

2.

If there were any
groundhogs, they
might see a faint
shadow today,

here in our mid-
winter spring,
moss on trees, just
like grass in driveway.

3.

I'm a man
with no pants,
open to
suggestion,

open to love,
old in an old world,
new at this, this
that you do.

4.

I'm living in
the future, put
out to pasture,
where I never thought
I'd be.

It's not an adventure,
I assure you, you
who don't generally
glance at the fields
beside your road.

5.

How soon they learned
you are among them
mine and theirs, and
when you are home, here.

This is where
I am, and here
you are, and among,
us among, us.

6.

You raised your hands,
pulled clouds away,
introduced
a bright blue,

as if you
were sent from the east
to do
this.

7.

There is nothing
so much to desire
as the Montreal
smile in your
photograph.

And if there is
a problem in composition
there is still the
picture, and you
are so much in it.

8.

My eyes say we
focus, say
we folk are
large in our lives,

say something of
us, you and I
subject of our
perspective.

9.

You are a
riddle of bones, a
rebus of what
I don't know, the sum

of all puzzling
I'm likely to
come see, come
saw, doctor.

10.

Pulled my pants
down in the kitchen,
what's, I said,
cooking?

        You al-
ready had a wooden
spoon in your hand,
devilish spice
in your grin.

11.

You. I remember
are grass, we are
grass, for all we
like to think
we think.

We are under
foot, fresh as the spring,
open to love, long
natural
love.

12.

The beasts of
the field shall
honour us, the
dragons and the owls

be our familiars,
kin to speak
our new tongue
with, seemly.

13.

Uncover thy locks,
make bare the leg,
uncover the thigh, pass
over the rivers.

Thy nakedness shall
be uncovered, yea,
would I be
thy ford.

14.

Would I be thy
Mercury, bring
message of
wisdom, or just
dumb, bring love

like a penitent, a
witch of a softening
heart left in
the damp over-
long, this song.

15.

You are on
your new ladder.
"She paints,"
I think, another
lovely poem

woman. Making
a wall pumpkin
in colour, relative
to a world full
of your hues.

16.

You tell me who
was popular
in my middle age,
I don't really

try to remember
the kind of September
you were born, it
was snowing, you said.

17.

I wish, you
are my well,
my deep
drink, my waking.

You wake and
my wish comes
true, my Eve,
my happy morn.

18.

I am a magpie,
you are swag,
is that our
word, in black
and white?

           I'm right,
I gather you to
my purposes, I
aim to hold
you down, and up.

19.

I am your clay,
you are the potter,
I am all awhirl,
you are, perhaps,
religious.

Or you were,
I am earth,
you are my
firmament, I am
perhaps, metaphorical.

20.

I was alone, no
birds in sight, in
an empty street,
feeling rueful.

You can't even
sing, but you lifted
this, feathers and all,
high, sky, lark.

21.

L'arc-en-ciel,
high colour, sky
bird, you do lift
my, what is it?

Spirit. You
manage to stop
my slouching to
that dark rookery.

22.

You hold up
at least
half the sky, I
climb under, lie
on my back.

The view, as
they say, flushes
my heart, is that
the right word, flushes
my old heart.

23.

Here's the wonder:
you hold up
the sky, while you
pull down
my pants.

You have us
coming through
laughter, leaving
the ess to
the nake.

24.

Leaving me naked
as a reptile, as
Egypt under
your body, sky

a net of stars,
a knot of light,
a neat trail
of my new prayer.

25.

No, not
an Eliot
in a basket
full.

      No asp-
irations in
that direction,
no coil.

26.

No pants, ass
naked as a
bend in the
road, no quest

but e-
scape, your grin
on line, on the side
I'm in.

27.

No quest, no
quail by
that road, you
follow?

        It's a
bird comes down
too easily, like
a simile.

28.

This bird,
do we need him
any more than
we need
ourselves?

You and I, we
fly
by the seat of
my pants.

Eggs in There

March

1.

I REMEMBER hearing my parents' voices in their bedroom, the rise and fall, quickness, slowing, but I heard no words. I knew what they were talking about, because it was bridge night. There had been three tables, two in our living room and one in the little dining room. In the morning I would hear the words, but not understand them. My father might say no trump. My mother might say grand slam.

2.

I REMEMBER my parents playing cards at the kitchen table at night. They had ashtrays, and my father made cigarettes with his mechanical cigarette roller—make one long long cigarette and use a razor blade to cut it into five regular cigarettes. Black Cat. I knew what they were doing but I didn't understand the arithmetic: fifteen two, fifteen four, fifteen six and a pair is eight. At least there with the cards in their hands they didn't say anything about finesse, or the rubber.

3.

I REMEMBER my parents doing some kind of calisthenics, circus, gymnastics, when I was a floor boy myself, my father lying on his back in slacks and white singlet undershirt, my mother in her white badminton shorts and white short-sleeved shirt, doing a handstand on his raised palms. Maybe he needed a shave or it was Saturday, of course, and I knew that in the high school gym, either of them could take a run and bounce off the springboard, go over the horse on their hands, and land thud thud, nicely on the mat.

4.

    I REMEMBER my mother and father mentioning the time my mother fell off a horse and landed hard on her head and knocked herself out, and for years and years I didn't know whether it was a gymnasium tumbling horse or a real animal horse, because I sort of knew that my mother had been brought up on a farm back in the hills, and when my father walked the hills to her place, he was ten years older than she, and there were her brothers sitting on the fence rail, with or without a rifle, probably without.

5.

I REMEMBER my Uncle Gerry giving my Auntie Pam's breast a cute hold and saying something friendly when I was staying with them in Kelowna. She was young and pretty and I was a twerp and I told her when she asked that I did need someone to wash my back in the bathtub. Uncle Gerry and Auntie Pam played cards with my parents a lot, usually bridge, all of them smoking from round cans and then a few years later from cubic boxes made of light cardboard. That was one of the changes that tipped me off that in the future the present would be chintzier than the past. When I started smoking I always bought tailor-mades.

6.

I REMEMBER the bottle of rye whiskey that was on the top shelf to the left of the sink. It was there for years. I don't remember my parents having a drink, though they went through coffee or vice versa like a teenager through sugar or vice versa. I don't remember them swearing, though my father the preacher's son did say "Judas Priest!" when he banged his thumb. I don't remember them dancing, though they played cards under the smoky air. I don't remember them fighting or arguing or shouting at each other, ever. In my lonely self I vowed never to do any of those things, and then I did them all.

7.

I REMEMBER going to church with my parents a few times. At my grandmother's funeral in West Summerland, where I used to go to church with her, I saw tears in my father's eyes, and I felt guilty for once again looking with sexual curiosity I suppose it was at a bovine pretty young woman in the choir. I wore my $30.00 suit, that came with an extra pair of trousers, at my grandfather's funeral in West Summerland, and I had my picture taken next to a fruit tree, a cigarette in my mouth, gel in my hair. At my father's funeral on the Ides of March in Oliver, at the United Church, I held my sister's hand and my mother's hand, and heard my father say, "It's all right." And I wished that it were.

8.

I REMEMBER being in the back seat, maybe with my sister, as my parents drove home in the darkness after a visit with my grandparents in West Summerland or my uncle and aunt in Naramata. Those were all Bowerings, and they were the ones who still lived in the Okanagan Valley, thirty-seven miles away or twenty-seven miles away if they were my aunt and uncle in Penticton. It was cold in the back of the car, so we were under a blanket, and I could see the aura of light from the dashboard or my parents' heads, my father in his Dick Tracy hat and my mother in a mother hat. There was always a clock on the dashboard but we never had a car that the clock worked in.

9.

    I REMEMBER my parents' visit to Montreal, their only trip ever to the east. We took them to Auberge St. Tropez, and my father surprised me, ordering the rabbit, and just two days ago my mother mentioned that she had surprised herself by ordering the salmon but was it really salmon, and now I recall that when I was in grade one we had a dead deer hanging head down in the back yard in Greenwood. In Montreal I took my father to Jarry Park, and he was a lifelong baseball fan but this was his only major league ball game, and so now when I go to ball games in St. Louis or Detroit, I do it for him but I do it for me too, and now I don't remember anywhere else we went in Montreal with my parents but I wonder whether my mother wanted to be there, so far from home, but I'll bet my father did.

10.

 I REMEMBER that in middle age, my parents took up golf. They also took up curling in later middle age, but I never saw them doing that. My mother was a methodical, good-sense golfer, and eventually she would get a hole-in-one, twice. My father was a fanatic, never-give-up person. If his drive sliced into the tall tulies across the road, you would see his head for half a second, as he jumped straight into the air to line up his next thrashing shot out of the reeds. In winter, if it snowed, he painted a few balls orange and made good use of his five iron. His drive was usually low and straight, as if he had figured it out scientifically.

11.

I THINK I REMEMBER my mother reaching over with her left hand and holding the steering wheel while my father rolled a cigarette and lit it. He must have been driving slowly on a straight stretch of road, though where we lived there weren't any really straight stretches. I am using adverbs to confuse any USAmerican readers. My mother liked to see how long she could grow a cigarette ash. At the kitchen sink, with the window open, she would be washing and drying, or more likely trying to take the peel off an apple all in one piece, and her cigarette would be more than half ash. We would hurry to her with an ashtray, humorously, but she had the sink and perhaps thoughts of a personal record-length cigarette ash. There are so many tricks, I later learned, that you can do with a cigarette.

12.

I REMEMBER a hallway at one end of which I was playing around or examining something on the floor. I was about three or four. At the other end of the hallway were doors, one on one side closing or opening a bedroom for adults, one on the other opening or closing a bathroom. This must have been when I was three, because the house we lived in when I was four had no bathroom. My mother, who was twenty-two or twenty-three, but probably twenty-two, was in the bathroom and needed to get to the bedroom. She was hoping to make such transit naked, so felt the need to be fast. Perhaps her clothes were all in the bedroom, but then she had a towel in the other. Probably she just thought that the likelihood of getting across the hall unseen meant that she needn't go to all the trouble of a towel. On the floor with my stuff, whatever it was, I lifted my head and looked down the hallway, to see my mother's naked leap, her surprising body in the air between two doors for a second or less.

13.

I REMEMBER my parents but especially my mother when it came to our chickens. We had chickens wherever we lived, and it struck me as peculiar when I met people who did not have chickens in their yard. We had white chickens and brown chickens and bantams. My father chopped the chickens' heads off with the same axe and chopping block he used for the stove wood and kindling. Chickens would run around the yard and crow with their heads gone. One I remember in Greenwood flew up and landed on the roof over the back porch. My mother would put the headless chicken into a bucket of boiling water, and I hated the smell of hot wet feathers. Then she would pluck the feathers out. I watched it all, either horrified or fascinated. Then the pimply blue-white chicken body would be lying on its back on the sinkboard, and my mother would reach in and pull out its insides. They were very shiny, purple and yellow, and sometimes there would be eggs in there, with no shells on them. My mother should have been my hero. My father was elsewhere.

14.

I REMEMBER that both my parents were catchers in softball, call it fastball. Apparently my father was a first baseman in baseball, but when I saw him he was wearing all that gear, mask, chest protector, shin guards. I never knew whether he wore a cup. There he was in his expert catcher's crouch, and I guess I saw my mother catching too, but she did that mainly to get near my father, who was the coach of the young women's team. My father had only the bottom half of the index finger on his throwing hand, but he could whip that ball. So when it came to Air Cadet camp in Abbotsford the summer I was fourteen, I was the catcher for the British Columbia team, and I threw out two baserunners in one inning. That was the highlight of my catching life.

15.

    I REMEMBER the wisdom of my mother when it came to my eighth birthday. Now, I never had a birthday party to which other kids came, at least not when I was still a kid. A day or two before I turned eight, my mother asked me whether I'd rather have a birthday cake or a birthday pie. As my birthday is December 1, and as we were living in an orchard, it would be apple pie. Even today I prefer pie to cake, but now that I can afford them, I don't get to eat either. But anyone in his right mind would choose pie, so I did. Then my mother asked me whether I wanted to eat the whole pie or share it with my parents and sister.

16.

I REMEMBER my father's sports stuff, his old baseball spikes I tried to wear but the metal hurt my feet, his old ice skates that were too tight and worn to a frazzle, his old black high top running shoes that he'd used in basketball games before I was born, and now the shoelaces were broken and too short. I didn't even try them on, afraid I'd fall into a time warp such as I was always reading about in the pages of *Fantasy & Science Fiction* magazine, edited by Anthony Boucher. My parents had old wooden badminton racquets. My mother wore a pleated white skirt, and my father wore the white slacks he also wore to his bi-weekly Elks meetings.

17.

AH, I REMEMBER my mother and her pie crust. This is the woman who tried to have a cigarette-long cigarette ash, who tried to peel an apple all in one piece of peel. I'd see her, the pie held up on the fingertips and thumb of her left hand, her right holding the long knife and trying to trim the circumference of the top crust in one long ribbon of dough. My father was so lucky. As my mother and I were discussing two weeks ago up in Canada on the phone, she did not like cherry pie with the usual pink and sour cherries, but rather fully ripe, almost black, Bings, not the type of store-bought cherry pie, but the wonderful Bing cherry pie that made all other cherry pies pale in comparison all my life through. I don't eat any pie now, but if I did, I might try to fulfill a life's ambition, and you know what that is.

18.

I REMEMBER the community sports day, though not what it was called, in Greenwood when I was in grade one and the year before that. I don't remember what my father did, though I remember his playing broomball in the winter, and I'll bet that he volunteered for a lot of the organizing. The events took place on the big playing fields in front of our hillside house. I do remember that for two years in a row my mother was the women's champion spike-driver. You had to hammer a spike all the way into a chunk of wood, meaning that you had to combine strength with good technique and dexterity. My mother was pretty good with a switch, too. It seemed the most normal thing in the world that my mother was the spike-driving champ.

19.

I REMEMBER my father writing a letter to his parents on the same day every week, and getting a letter from them on the same day every week. We lived in Oliver, and they lived in West Summerland, thirty-seven miles away. Later, I would note that my friend Tony wrote to his parents in Australia once a week on the same day. It must have been an English thing, or a British Empire kind of thing. Lately I have got into the habit of telephoning my mother once a week, always on the same evening. But I do not remember her writing to her parents every week on the same day, or at all, really, though maybe she did sometimes. They lived over in the Kootenays, and for a while in Greenwood, maybe a hundred or a hundred-and-fifty miles away.

20.

I REMEMBER that it was always kept in mind that my father was ten years older than my mother. Not kept in mind to explain anything, just one of a million facts that I enjoyed knowing when I was a kid, like the fact that Mars has two moons. Ewart and Pearl were my parents, so they were a couple of people who were comfortably older than I, not really old, I mean that I was in a little shock when it became apparent that my father was turning fifty. I didn't go around being aware that my mother was nineteen when I was born, a year or so out of school. My father was one of the schoolteachers. I thought for a long time that that made us normal, that all dads were a little older than moms, maybe ten years.

21.

I DON'T REMEMBER my parents' ever celebrating their wedding anniversary, because they were married on Boxing Day. There's a present my dad never exchanged. So when I was born they had been married for eleven months, more or less. I guess that their wedding anniversary was a part of Christmas and New Year's. Here is the main story I heard about their wedding: Uncle Gerry, who was a young pup, did something funny with their luggage, and then when the bridal couple's car drove away, he exclaimed that the job had backfired, because whatever was supposed to happen had happened to his own suitcase instead. I wish that I could remember the details. It all sounds like an André Gide novel.

22.

I REMEMBER that there wasn't much in the way of music in my parents' house, until I bought my little 45 rpm changer. They never had a gramophone. When we house-sat the Zarellis' house for a summer, I played all Mr. Zarelli's 78 rpm Enrico Caruso and Guy Lombardo records over and over. At our house there were some radios, but I think that I was the only person to listen to music on them. I was also the only family member with an instrument, and as it was the school's tuba, I hardly ever brought it home. My father used to sing, though, in his copyright EHB voice, not to be confused with a tenor or a baritone or Dennis Day, whom my mother loved when he sang his song on the Jack Benny show on Sunday night. My father sang the same songs always—"Oh, My Darling Nellie Grey," and "I Wear My Pink Pyjamas," etc. I don't remember my mother singing, but as she said on the telephone last week, "Sing 'Danny Boy,' and you'll have me crying."

23.

I REMEMBER my father and me having competing teams. It used to make me wonder, to know that he was a fan of the Giants, say, long before I was born, in his own life story. My kid brothers are both Montreal Canadiens fans, and I don't understand that, because the Canadiens were my father's team. I took him to see them in Vancouver, the first time in his life, which never did get long enough. He was a Canadiens fan, and I don't know why, because in rural British Columbia we were pretty well all Toronto Maple Leafs fans, though my uncle Gerry was somehow a Boston Bruins fan. So it was my dad's Habs versus my Leafs, It was his Giants versus my Dodgers. My father, who took a bar of soap into the lake. His Indians versus my Red Sox. No football, no basketball. You had to have a team, and stay with them and be serious about it. Except for my mother. She has always rooted for whatever team is playing against your team, for the competition, even if it was the New York Yankees.

24.

I REMEMBER that my parents drank coffee all day long, and until recently, so did I. So did my late wife and I. So does my sister, a year younger than I; she has a pot on all day. But she still smokes cigarettes. About the time I stopped smoking cigarettes, I cut my coffee down to about three cups a day. Uncle Gerry and Auntie Pam downed it all day and night.
I have always known that coffee is a family habit, but my daughter didn't get it. What I really liked was getting old enough to have coffee with my parents, and smoke cigarettes with them. My father always put one drop of milk into his coffee. He hated milk.

25.

I REMEMBER my parents trying to make "potato champagne." I guess it was a fad of the time. Here was a couple who would go a year without having a drink—maybe my father would have a beer in the hot orchard if everyone else was holding a long-necked bottle of Princeton Lager, with condensation on it. Now here was a big pot or something in the fridge, raisins floating on some liquid. I had a sip when no one else was home, and I don't remember enjoying it. I also don't remember my parents' drinking potato champagne. My mother probably wound up pouring it out on the tomato plants in the back yard.

26.

I REMEMBER my parents working all their days. They didn't have a summer vacation till my father Ewart was in his sixties. Then they went to the Salton Sea to golf a few times. The last time they did it, my father came home to Canada and died. My father was a high school teacher and my mother was a housewife, but they were always working. He worked in orchards, at the cannery, at the box factory, on the highway, at the Rock Creek bridge. My mother worked at a flower shop or giving perms, but more often at the sorting belt in a packing house. In the fall my father would come home from teaching, change duds, and go pick apples till dark, or past dark if they had lights. They had to work, and they did.

27.

I REMEMBER my parents reading all the time, especially before television arrived and I was gone. I don't remember, particularly, what my mother liked to read, though now in her ninetieth year, she reads large-print novels one after another, books from the Oliver library, by authors I have never heard of. In the old days, my father, who is in his one hundredth year now but gone, read the novel that was published in the *Star Weekly*, condensed books, they may have been. His favourite author was Erle Stanley Gardner, so later I read about fifteen of his cases. His other favourite author was Thorne Smith, who was kind of risqué. In those days my favourite author was Max Brand, and my other favourite author was Zane Grey. My father loved the newspaper and so did I. I started reading the Vancouver *Province* when I was four, I guess.

28.

I REMEMBER being glad that my parents had names that the other kids' parents did not have. Ewart and Pearl. That's what people said. I didn't even notice that they rimed, not particularly. I was not crazy about my stodgy old name, but I thought it was interesting that my grandfather and father and I all had the same middle name—Harry. My grandfather went by that name because his first name was Jabez. He pronounced Harry differently because he still had English habits of speech. I can't even say Harry the way English people do. One of my favourite writers was Zane Grey. He took the name Zane from his mother. His real first name was Pearl. He was a nice colour, I used to think.

29.

I REMEMBER my mother saying after my father died, "He was too young." She lived with him for less than forty years, and now she has lived without him for more than thirty years. While he was dying in California and Vancouver, she scarcely left his side, at our underfurnished house, then at Jamie Reid's mother Eunice's apartment near the hospital, then at the hospital. She spent the days and nights with him, in love like an eighteen-year-old girl. He never got to be the age I am now, and she is still alive, Pearl. I went on an eastern reading trip while he was dying, but my mother was devotion. I was not amazed, but I could have been.

30.

 I REMEMBER getting letters from my father, and then after he died, getting letters from my mother. My father always wrote on small linen with small even words leaning forward, followed by his signature, very tidy, and, I thought, maybe scientific. My mother wrote on whatever paper she had to hand, often pages torn from a notebook with coil binding, so that her pages had broken circles on their edges. Her words leaned every which way, and featured crossings-out or words poked in above other words, or questions such as "that doesn't look right, does it?" But they were both good spellers, and knew how to make a sentence. People did back then, whether they were schoolteachers or hillbillies. Now I phone my mother on Sunday evenings. She doesn't think that she has anything to write.

31.

    I DON'T REMEMBER my parents' coming to the auditorium when I acted on stage, skinny kid being Wilde's "Earnest" or a Brontë fop, a burglar or a Nazi officer, an animal or an Englishman. I don't remember their attending when I played tuba in the high school band, or when I sang the bass clef in the high school choir. I don't remember seeing them in the gymnasium when I was playing for the high school volleyball team, or in the grandstand when I played my few games of baseball. Who knows whether they read my articles in the Oliver *Chronicle* and the Penticton *Herald*? How would you know? I don't know whether they went to the Community Hall to see my giant cartoon portraits of all the firemen. I don't know whether they ever saw me marching with the Air Cadets. I don't remember their ever coming to anything, but I guess they did.

U.S. Sonnets

April

1. The puppy

The puppy lies flat on its side,
making it easier for the little girl

using a piece of white chalk
to draw an outline of the dead dog

on the mostly flat section
of broken concrete, some old floor

it appears to be, perhaps of a
factory that has been torn down

in all likelihood before the little girl
was born, certainly long before the dog,

a fuzzy creature, black and white
toes and a line of white on its chest,

maybe two months old. The little girl
is just finishing the chalk outline.

2. "The American

"The American Society for the Defense of
Tradition, Family and Property was formed

to resist, in the realm of ideas, the liberal,
socialist and communist trends of the times.

Jesus was not homosexual, and his disciples
were straight. Brazil says no to gun control.

We denounce the use of fiction to spread error.
Something similar to what happens in

Communist countries is developing
in San Francisco. The soldier had grown up

and matured while the students were off
to play. The followers of President Chávez

make patent the link between the radical left
and a Satanic hatred."

3. We see

We see the police officer from a rear
three-quarter view. He is hatless, in police

pants and short-sleeved shirt, emblem on
his sleeve, dark glasses on his face, an

automatic pistol in both hands. His slacks
drape nicely over his leather police shoes.

His automatic pistol is pointed at a young man
in baggy pants and green tee-shirt, athletic

shoes. He has, as he has been instructed, got
out of his SUV, the door of which is open.

He is standing with his head tilted back
because he is draining the last of a can of beer.

We do not know the nature of the offense
of which he is suspected, nor do we care.

4. Jews For

Jews For the Preservation of Firearms Possession
tell us that U.S. gun laws are based upon

the German Nazi Weapons Law of March 18,
1938, which cleared the way for World War Two

and Nazi genocide against the Jews, Gypsies
and seven million other people. That's thirteen million

Holocaust victims, and more to come. The Eugenics
movement that ended in Hitler's death camps

began here with liberal, educated do-gooders. In
the good old Bill of Rights days, you could sit up

in the back of an open convertible and feel the
wind in your face without being fined for a

seat-belt violation. You could get on an airplane
carrying a firearm for self-defense.

5. The chromium

The chromium handrails flash in sunlight that
shines as well on the red tiles of the Fitness

Center toward which the up escalator leads,
upon which stand two young men in shorts.

There is also a down escalator, and between
the two escalators a flight of fifteen stairs

upon which no one is stepping. One of the
young men is carrying a bag from a fast

food outlet. This is, according to a red, white
and blue sign, a 24-hour Fitness Center. The sign

bears the same colours as the Star of David signifying
Jews for the Preservation of Firearms. The red tiles

suggest southern California, where there is sometimes
an unfortunate association of firearms with fast food.

6. "July 4

"July 4, 1776, we states write in declaring
separation from that wretched king because he

has affected to render the Military independent of
and superior to the Civil Power, quartering large

bodies of armed troops among us. Well, we cannot
let that happen. He has excited domestic insurrections

among us, our servants and slaves begin to believe
they are endowed with certain inalienable rights, we

cannot hang them all. He has endeavoured to bring on
the inhabitants of our frontiers, the merciless Indian

Savages whose known rule of warfare, is an undistinguished
destruction of all ages, sexes and conditions. We

will have to expand our frontiers, and for the king's monsters
reserve terrible land where they may perish unseen by our eyes."

7. It is

It is a metal flask with a kind of silvery
shine, curved a little to fit into a rear pocket,

decorated on the front with a Confederate States
of America flag, that outlaw motorcycle gangs and

Southern politicians like to exhibit, thirteen white
stars on X-shaped bars, the same number of rebel

stars on Betsy Ross's rebel flag in 1776. Betsy
was a business person and so is the patriot selling

this flask, who advises: "Keep your liquor cold and
out of sight with this new 602 Confederate Flag

Flask. A flask is perfect for use in restaurants when
you do not want to pay those high alcohol prices.

Order a regular Coke and when the waiter goes away
you can add six ounces of your favorite alcohol beverage."

8. José, does

José, does that star-spangled banner yet wave,
o'er the home of the Turks, and the land of the

Cubans, and the land of the Greeks, and the land
of the Spanish, and the land of the Belgians, and the

land of the Koreans, and the land of the Germans, and the
land of the Japanese, and the land of the Saudis, and

the land of the Italians, and the land of the Dutch,
and the land of the Puerto Ricans, and the land of

the Icelanders, and the land of the Diego Garcians, and
the land of the Bahrainis, and the land of the

Portuguese, and the land of the Brits, and the land
of the Iraqis, and the land of the Afghanis, and the

land of the Panamanians, and the land of the Filipinos,
and the land of the Kiowa, Apache, Lakota and Sioux?

9. It looks

It looks as if we are at some Southern rural place
with pickup trucks parked under the trees, a

shadowed building with corrugated tin roof. In the
centre of the picture is a USAmerican muscle car,

a Thunderbird or Camaro or Barracuda or Mustang,
but this one has been worked on for hundreds of hours,

and it is as they say down there, real long, real low,
and real colourful, mainly metallic blue with yellow

lightning bolts, and along the side in yellow lightning
is the name Shirl Greer. The tires are huge, with

deep shiny wheels, and there are ominous bumps
on the long hood. On this side of the machine is a big

young fat man in a white tee shirt, denim shorts and
athletic footwear. On the other side, a fat guy in teal and denim.

10. "Saturday morning

"Saturday morning Prayer Breakfast. Don't miss this
opportunity for fellowship and sharing with your NRA

family. Dave Butz, former All-Pro defensive tackle with
the Washington Redskins, will be Keynote Speaker. Bring

your whole family to see acres of the latest guns
and gear. Ensure victory in this year's elections.

Show your NRA support by shopping at Amazon.com.
Tom Marx, former Chicago police officer and an

instructor for the Smith & Wesson Academy, teaches all
aspects of concealed carry for men and women. Arm

yourself with protection at the NRA-endorsed Insurance
program. Or contact Century International Arms, Inc.

for an Original Nazi War Medal, 1939. We are the National
Rifle Association, America's oldest civil rights organization."

11. We've grown

We've grown used to team mascots, guys or sometimes
women, dressed up as cartoon animals or birds or something

you don't know about, with giant feet. Here is Eddie
Eagle, big smiling mascot of the National Rifle Ass.,

his huge wing-hands around the ribs of two little girls,
daughters of the NRA family, one has to guess. He has

big happy eyes and eagle dimples, and his name is
spelled in white capitals across his brisket. Like

safety lessons concerning swimming pools, electrical
outlets, matchbooks and household poisons, Eddie Eagle's

safety lesson is one that children should not miss.
That's what it says here. Guns are just like

swimming pools and matchbooks. Except that
if you're killing, say, an eagle, a gun would be quicker.

12. "Dear Friend

"Dear Friend: This message has been sent to you by
a friend or relative who has recently disappeared

along with millions and millions of people around the world.
The reason they chose to send you this letter is because

they cared about you and would like you to know the truth
about where they went. This may come as a shock to you,

but the one who sent you this has been taken up to
Heaven. I am sure that there will be a lot of speculation

as to what happened to all these people. The theories
of some scientists and world leaders will have so much

credibility that most of the world will believe them. It will
sound like the truth! But, there is only one truth. And,

that truth is that Jesus Christ took with him to Heaven
all who believed in Him and made Him their Lord."

13. Under one

Under one of those big thick branching-out trees
you expect to see in the U.S. South, a station wagon

Jeep is parked on the tidy grass. A couple of feet
from the Jeep is a big tall sign demanding NO PARKING,

NO DRIVING ON GRASS. There is a thick wood full of oaks
in the background, and a paved roadway just beyond

the grass, twenty-five meters away. Inside the Jeep are
four gentle old people, the gents in the front, the ladies

in the back. The nice old gent behind the wheel is
wearing his summer weight straw fedora. There are no

junk food wrappers on the grass beside the Jeep. I'll
bet those people are waiting for the Rapture. I'll

bet they're leaving four of those Rapture letters for
relatives who will wonder about their abandoned Jeep.

14. "Unless the

"Unless the UFO is surrounded by a force field to
vaporize the slugs, you are going to cause some serious

damage to the craft and its inhabitants. Maybe if
we shoot up a few of them, they (whoever they are)

will rethink their game plan. Don't let anyone or
anything take you inside a craft that has landed.

You aren't required to follow. Think and act as
the aggressor rather than as a prisoner. You don't

have to give any of your body parts to anyone if
you don't want to. You don't have to give your

planet to anyone if you don't want to. Shoot first
and ask questions later. At this stage of the game

I believe we shoot, shoot them down. The more
damage you can cause, the better for our side."

15. Now, here

Now, here are some clean-cut fairly young white men
staging a demonstration against something, most

in golf shirts, one in a suit and tie, blow-dried
hair such as TV preachers wear. Some wear glasses,

one has a tidy moustache, and many of them are
carrying signs, most of these hand-lettered, as if

they were the spectators at a TV wrestling show.
Most of their signs you can't really read. One has a

religious cross in the corner. One has a word ending
"tery," and another a word ending "ery." I wonder

whether these men are amassed to oppose mystery, or
maybe the use of a psaltery. One sign is clearly readable.

It commands: "Teach our children Reading, Writing
Arithetic Not Gambling." It doesn't add up, I say.

16. Thomas Jefferson

Thomas Jefferson, Architect of Democracy, wrote:
"I have sworn upon the altar of God my Hostility

against every form of tyranny over the mind of man ….
The blacks, whether originally a distinct race, or made

distinct by time and circumstances, are inferior to the
whites in the endowments both of body and mind ….

I candidly confess that I have ever looked on Cuba as
the most interesting addition which could be made to

our system of states …. If we seize Cuba we will be
masters of the Caribbean. We should then have only

to include the north in our Confederacy …. We shall
form to the American union a barrier against the dangerous

extension of the British province of Canada and add
to the Empire of liberty an extensive and fertile Country."

17. In this

In this photograph by Jacob Holdt the two white men are
looking away from us along the sidewalk, and the two

black boys are looking down. The two white men are
wearing suits and ties, and where they are looking,

there in the dappled sunlight, white women in high
boots are walking to and fro from the stores. The two

black boys are looking down because that is their work.
They are wearing short-sleeved shirts and dungarees and

sneakers. One of the white men is wearing oxfords, and
the other is wearing short boots with heels. They have

this footwear resting on tilt-top boxes, and the boys
are polishing their footwear. One can guess that at least

one of these white men has recently sworn on the altar
of God his hostility against every form of tyranny.

18. The Aryan

The Aryan Nations of Idaho ask: "Martin Luther King,
Civil Rights Leader or Sexual Pervert? His Dream was

the product of a syphlitic mind that desired the destruction,
(by race mixing) of his Race of whom he was ashamed,

& also of the White Race who he hated because he was
not a member of it. Evidence proved King was under

direct orders of Soviet spies & financed by the Communist
Party. In New York City King got drunk & threatened

a young White girl working for civil rights, to submit
to his strange sexual tastes or he would jump from the

13th floor window! She succumed to prove her loyalty to
King. Washington's old Willard Hotel was the scene of King

forcing White women to drink 'Black Russians.' Is this the kind
of person we should hold up to our children as a National hero?"

19. Jacob Holdt

Jacob Holdt took a series of photographs of a family
of Ku Klux Klanspeople. They hold hands around the

table, saying Grace in their Klan robes, for example. In
this one, the mom, I forget her name, is talking on a

cordless phone, which she holds to her left ear. She
is wearing a brown sweater big enough to belong to

her husband. She has long curled hair piled on her head
and hanging down her back. We can see behind her

the kitchen stove and a white microwave oven, and dishes
drying in a rack. Over the little kitchen window is a

Venetian blind, and over the top half of the Venetian blind
a taffeta curtain with gatherings across the top. On the

counter in front of her there is a hammer, a package of
cigarettes, a roll of tape, and the KKK hood she is ironing.

20. Many, many

Many, many times I have heard this question, "Is anyone ever totally healed from homosexuality?"

Typically, it comes from someone who himself or herself is struggling with homosexuality, and has

not achieved the level of healing or growth that he or she had hoped for. Then what is a reasonable

expectation for healing from same-sex attraction (SSA)? Of course we minister to people who are not there

yet. One other missing ingredient is often present in former SSA men; they don't lust after women like

other men do. Of course, God is not in the business of dealing out lust. It seems that God, more often

than not, moves more slowly than we would like Him to. Please pray for Regeneration.

21. The star-spangled

The star-spangled banner fills a lot of catalogues,
covers a lot of contingencies, whose broad

stripes and bright stars Jack Kerouac refused to sit
upon, the red white and blue a bangle for your

wrist, a strangle for your necktie. But here is one
I was really hoping for, a classic USAmerican gee-

string, available in models for the female or male
gee. The one I'm looking at in full colour reproduction

shows a comely white male from just below his
belly button to just above his knees, a bright rect-

angle, and just in the middle the briefest of patriotic
undies, red and white stripes on one side, white stars

on a blue sky to the other; it's enough to make you
stand at attention, open your heart, and sing, string, sing.

22. "I want

"I want you to know that I am participating in
the boycott of Ford Motor Company. I ask that you

pass along to Ford Motor Company chairman Bill Ford
my concern regarding Ford's support for the homo-

sexual agenda, including financial contributions to
groups promoting homosexual marriage. On a

recent episode of CBS's *Without a Trace*, Ford proved
to the homosexual community the company's commitment

to their agenda. The Ford-sponsored program included
a scene of two lesbians passionately kissing each other.

Ford defines 'family' to include homosexual and
lesbian couples. Warning: many will find these photos

offensive. We include them only to show the type of
activity Ford feels deserves their official sponsorship."

23. It's a

It's a hot summer's day somewhere; everyone is
wearing shorts. There's a kid in that uniform, tee

shirt, yellow shorts, white socks, sneakers. There's a guy
beside him, fat legs between white socks and shorts.

Behind them there's a USAmerican flag, a woman
taking a picture, another woman with her hands on her

hips. She's wearing tee shirt and shorts. She's overweight.
In the middle, up front, in the centre of this picture,

is a guy in shorts and a St. Louis Cardinals tee shirt.
He's wearing the stars and stripes around his head, long

hair hanging down in thin twists. He's got narrow sun-
glasses and a thin mustache. He is carrying two hand-lettered

signs. The one held low says GO USA. In his other hand
he holds up a sign that says Get A BRAIN! MORANS.

24. At P.O.

At P.O. Box 362, Hayden, Idaho 83835, they
warn us about Jewish Propaganda, Hypocritical

—Evil—With Malice Aforethought. They tell us that
"Sumner Redstone, top Jew at Paramount Pictures &

MTV Films says 'White girls, it's OK to have
sex with Blacks: in fact, it's real cool! Just

say yes! Your not prejudice are you?' To shield
Jewish children, 'yeshiva' schools are being built,

where the chosen children will be taught to honor their
culture and pass it along to the next generation.

Jews have plans for our children too. WHITE children
will be conditioned for death, taught to disavow

their 'racist' culture and accept assimilation. Warn
your children about the Jews." Aryan Nations.

25. The smallish

The smallish animal, whatever it was,
lies flat on its side, more or less, or

maybe on its belly. Anyway, we can see
a tail and two short legs and that

might be the remains of a face under the
yellow paint. We are in the middle of what

we up here call North America, let's say
a worn down unimportant back road paved

highway, two rough lanes on either side.
There's some kind of SUV driving away

from us, a pickup truck approaching. The
double yellow line down the middle of the

road is not exactly straight but it is new paint,
and this dead critter wears two yellow stripes.

26. "Help us

"Help us teach American Youth the Truth—
with music! The youth in America are being

lied to by liberal politicians and the mainstream
media ... but we've come up with a Great

way to get the Truth to them: Music. The
Right Brothers, a conservative music duo out of

Nashville, has released a new song that does
what needed to be done: it tells the truth. Titled

'Bush was Right,' the song hits the listener with
fact after *fact* after *fact*—but the tune is so

catchy, and the music is so driving, you can't
help but sing along (especially on the chorus)!

>Bush was right!
>Bush was right!
>Bush was right!"

27. In Jacob

In Jacob Holdt's photo we are looking at
a building that appears to be a big shed. It

has uneven pieces of asphalt shingle on its
wall, and the opened door is weathered

boards with other boards nailed across it. A
triangle of sunlight reveals a bit of old

furniture, so this is probably a dwelling. In front
of the door are a couple of broken wooden steps

and beside them are broken boards coming off the
structure, plus the remains of a blasted little

tree trunk. Standing on the top step, facing us,
with no smile on her face, is a thin old woman

in a home-made dress, lisle stockings on swollen
legs, and, oh yes, she's carrying a very long revolver.

28. "Do you

"Do you wish to honor God? Then you must support the death penalty. If the death penalty is not for

today, then why didn't Paul tell us? Did you know that God has actually promised to BLESS us if we

follow His plan of using the death penalty? God WANTS to bless our nation, but He can't do it with killers

running loose or with them sitting in prison receiving free meals. That's insane! I cannot honestly ask God

to bless America while we allow such wickedness to prevail. I bet 18,000 executions would deter some

crime! I personally think we need TELEVISED executions every night at 8:00 p.m. How does the death penalty help

the environment? God's word can answer that. Pollution is associated with SIN, not carbon monoxide."—James L. Melton.

29. In Jacob

In Jacob Holdt's photo we see a short man
in brown slacks and a striped shirt, who is

carrying women's furs in both hands. They
could be stoles or short jackets, and they

could be mink or ermine. He is walking toward
our left, and checking out the scene. The scene

involves a policeman in a short-sleeved shirt
who has his left shoe up on a step, his right on

the sidewalk, and he appears to be holding a
notebook and a pencil, looking down at them, preparing

to write. Slung low on his narrow hips are his
accoutrements, pistol, baton, mace, etc. He and the

fur-carrying man are white, as they say. The man
or woman lying dead or alive on the sidewalk? Who knows?

30. "We believe

"We believe the White, Anglo-Saxon, Germanic and kindred people to be God's true, literal children of Israel. This

chosen seedline making up the 'Christian Nations' (Gen. 35:11) of the earth stands superior to all other peoples in their

call as God's servant race. We believe in an existing being known as the Devil or Satan and called the Serpent, who

has a literal 'seed' or posterity in the earth (Gen. 3:15) commonly called Jews today. We believe that the Man Adam

is father of the White Race only. Race-mixing is an abomination in the sight of Almighty God. Homosexuality is an abomination

before God and should be punished by death (I Cor. 6:9). We believe that the United States fulfills the prophesied place

(Ezek. 36:24) where Christians from all the tribes of Israel would be regathered. It is here in this blessed land (Deut. 15:6)."

Montenegro 1966

May

Calgary

In the Calgary International Airport
throngs of German Alberta peasants,
men wearing blue straw fedoras,
women broad as pantry doors

joined Tony and Lorna and me. I blew a kiss
from the dramatic screen actor hero
entrance to the DC6, what a safe
plane, full of German words and baby screams.

I took off my boots over the pack ice
and the stewardess could see holes in my socks.
I could see a stick of gum in her breast
pocket—Juicy Fruit, it said. So went my wit
in 1966.

      There's a swimsuit in my suitcase
and the Mediterranean up ahead, but we're
on the ground at Keflavik. Iceland smells
like fish and there are U.S. sailors.

      Later in Düsseldorf I stood
across the street from my first Cinzano sign,
watching fluffy dogs on expensive leashes.

Aachen

Düsseldorf is glass and Mercedes, gleam of industrial
Rhine, with one little green bird
eating bugs, here with me under a bush
in the diesel city.
                      But then in Tony's new white 1966
Volkswagen we autobahn south, every other driver
at controls of a Stukka, hazy Krupp chimneys
along the great river, I remember last summer's
Mexico, *Óle, mein Herr.*
                      A lone woman leaning
on her hoe saw us, remembering a sigh in the
bomb shelter. After Coca Cola in Aachen
there were thousands of cows lying in soft battlefields,
Belgium, a priest raised his glum hand,
hello, or God bless?
                      History names flash by
like telephone poles in Saskatchewan, girls on bicycles
ride knock-kneed so you can't look up their skirts.

Calais

We departed Bruges in early morning, met
buses filled with school children grasping
Union Jacks—they're going to meet Queen Liz

but we're going to *her* country. "Allez,"
said the Belgian customs man around his cigarette,
nothing, said the French one. In Calais

they won't give English money for Belgian francs,
and on the ferry they won't accept French money.
The ferry is named *S.S. Free Enterprise.*

>I kneeled at the bow
>to see the actual
>white banks, oh patriarchs,
>oh Plantagenets!

"Left side of the road," murmured Tony as he
drove onto Blighty, "Left side of the road,"

beside which, beyond some lambs, I saw
two women in tweeds, carrying sticks,
striding a green field in Kent.

I was home at last,
lost.

Chichester

Imagine Chichester Cathedral,
                                  walk on corpses under stone;
no, churches are not where you praise life,
they store the dead;
                  let me not to the funeral of true minds
admit impediment.
                  Crazy William Collins knew
How sleep the Brave, who sink to Rest,
By all their Country's Wishes blest!

My eye included a lovely grim metaphor for
Mary Cramborne, gone May 9, 1722: "who through y^e
spotted Veil of ye Small p^{ox} rendered a pur^e and
unfpotted Soul to God."

                  I saw her neighbours' descendants,
ladies on bicycles with straw baskets hanging in front,
handlebars held seriously.

Then into the George we went, my first English pub!
I ambled to the bar in my denims, ordered bitter and lager.
Got some thrupp'ny bits.

London

"The one who sent you this has been taken
up to Heaven,"
 or is it up to London, first up
some downs in Sussex, then Epsom north
of Blake's cottage in Felpham, my favourite English
poet, naked and portly, oh Sacred grove!
 But that
was yesterday.

 Today we were seeking the Finnish poet,
Anselm, I said
hello, talked louder, Anselm talked louder and faster, Tony
cleared up some points.
 I loved this visit, we were
the Hollo men.
 Later Anselm and Josephine and Matti
Rossi the other Finnish poet, drank red paisano wine,
debating Venezuela and the state of the novel
till three in the morning.

 I blew out the candle
and someone
 blew out my brain.

London Bridge

We hied straight for Poets' Corner
to stand over the bones of gone minstrels,
be they for an age or for all time.

I stamped my pretty boot
       over the head of Lord Tennyson,
       but wait, isn't he in the dirt
       of the Isle of Wight? No reply.

At the National Gallery I knelt
       in front of Rembrandt for fifteen minutes.
I was thirty years old.
       This was my first time in civilization.

Then outside, there are fewer things better
       than to eat an apple in the sunshine,
       throw the core into the Thames.

. . . .

That night, after ample dark beer
       we walked over a bridge where Anselm
wrote "¡Cuba sí! ¡Eliot no!" on a spatter
       of bird lime.

The Tate

    I blew my nose and filled my handkerchief
with soot from London's blackened churches.
    Blake's people have huge Tate eyes, eyes
of men stoning a victim in anger.
    Watching telly with Anselm's kids, how they enjoy
me, imagining hairy goggle Allen Ginsberg in this house betimes,
    spooking around with finger cymbals, the kids
shuddering in their livers.

    Around the corner the little church where Missouri
Traveler, Tea S. Eliot dreamt his Anglican poems.

    I sat back and smoked confidently on the train, small
town boy sophisticate in Empire's centre, old
    after his time, got off at Leicester Square,
music in his head.

    Alack! the night comes on, and the high winds
Do sorely ruffle

                    us home to London, S.W. 7.

Fleet Street

In the corner Lyons café
                         under the bullying stare
of a fat old dame with tugboat accent
I feasted on
manhole coffee,
two mousemeat sausages, and
a wimpled fiberglass egg
on a piece of roofing shingle.

It cost several shillings.
I wished I had eaten the money.

That night after my poetry reading at Better Books
they gave me five pounds,
saving me from cashing another traveller's cheque.

And bitter English beer
helped my stomach forget.

Essex

In a roadside pub on the A12
      we enjoyed sour cow cream with coffee flavouring
and a blotter sandwich.
      The British at their leisure
must be thoroughly miserable, swim
      in the North Sea in March, at
pebbled beaches, pump warm air
      into packed theatres. Their toilet paper
is flexible glass. When an English child is born
      she is swaddled in sandpaper.
It provides the character that won the British Empire
      and invented the wing collar.

At Wivenhoe they gobble their jellied eels.
      spending lunch hour in a dark alley
with a scuffed soccer ball.

But in one crooked little town
      we passed under a row of hanging bells
that will brush the top of a truck
      too high to pass under the bridge up ahead.

Dover Castle

In Germany they drive like a spindled
      Luftwaffe, death merchants of the macadam; here
in Green Blighty these boxy little bumper-cars
      scarcely bend a weed as they roll their winding ways.

Dover Castle, tidy and spare, stands atop the
      highest part of those white cliffs, where there
should be a wind-tossed woman with grieving breast
      My first castle! No clattering hoofs, no
staircase sword fights.

      But I strode around like Hamlet for a while,
alone among breezy parapets, slipping into modern
      superior commonwealth postures at the stony beach
of St. Margarets at Cliffe, watching Brit families
      training their children in English hardihood and grim
enjoyment, dragging them with their brave tears along
      the olde icy strand.

Joan of Arc

The landscape of Europe is made
by the hands of men. Let's see—
a field here, and we'll put a miniature
forest there. Presto.

                We're in farm country,
black and white cows lying among yellow flowers.
Not the grapes of the south, but the cheeses,
I guess, of the north.

                Lille was the ugliest,
unpronounceable Reims the most beautiful
city we've seen. When we stop there's an old man
with white Van Dyke beard resting on a cane,
sitting on a bench across from the cathedral.

Joan's body is in the attitude of love, but
vertical, on a horse, sword in hand, legs
stretched wide. Tony and I came to grips
with our English backgrounds.

Cézanne and Monet

Walking hilly streets in my twelve-year-old sneakers,
I can feel cobbles on my soles.
                                    We're in Langres,
whereof Diderot did say

> *Les habitants de Langres*
> *ont de l'esprit, de*
> *l'education, de la gaieté,*
> *de la vivacité, et*
> *le parler traînant.*

Then we stopped to eat beside a creek
in a field of flowers, bread and oranges in the sun.

I took my shirt off for the first time. Tony had a
tiny green bug baby, with black eyes, on the back of his hand.

The painters failed to express this place, their luminosity
we love so; now each leaf was single in its portion of sun

and our words too failed, and Tony knew this as I said it,
and an hour ago we'd seen straight and pretty legs
on the young girls of Langres.

                                    Paul Cézanne said
    the progress to be made is endless.

Geneva

It's the Alps, we sensed the frontier,
      lovely European word of rhapsodic Thirties
           spy movies with moonlit ringlets and
stuffed railroad coach seats.

      Tony's on the trail of Madame de Staël, here
           where rainclouds hung over Lake Geneva, a man
is spread-legged, back to highway, having a restful leak
      while his truck waits.

           At the château
Goethe and Schiller, maybe Shelley and Mary, were in
      but the gate was locked. Monday again. We stood
           under the slight rain. Tony defied Napoleon.

In Geneva the workmen swept up red blossoms. In
      the café our little sandwiches were under plastic,
           ducks were forbidden to excrete in the park.

But in Chamonix we bunked with Percy Shelley,
      flew far in dread, our work and dwelling
           vanishing, like smoke before the tempest's stream.

Inside Mt. Blanc

Tony walked into a sloping meadow, secret
             camera behind his back, to snap
             his longed-for mountains,
cows jangling their bells all around him
             among the mayflowers.

But men kill themselves all over these white peaks,
planes crash into Mt. Blanc, steep cablecars snap,
machines fail and human corpses sprinkle the snow.

             I fidgeted for eleven kilometers
             under the highest volcano in Europe,
             offering my life
             to suicidal French and Italian tunnellers, till

we crossed to sunny Italy in the dark.

And drove up St. Bernard Pass till snow and snow trucks
stopped us, got out, traipsed high in the sky's ground.

I poked my finger into an ant hill
             till an ant trod my hand,
             a snail passed my slow foot,
             and in a pool of melted snow
             a cluster of eggs
             waited to be born,
             dreaming the far down ocean.

Two Jolly Men in Verona

In the Roman amphitheatre
  two scrawny cats, looking for miniature Christians,
and two Calgary lads, taking the sun.
  It's 505 feet across its axis—Verona
must have had a major-league team,

I was still thinking, slurping Pepsi under an umbrella,
watching my first bouncing, rolling Italian women,
  their breasts loose and heavy inside cotton or silk,
  or parakeet feathers, sway, I fell from my slight chair.

But Dante nearly brought me to my knees
  in an old and beautiful square, ringed
  on rooftops by lesser poets, Dante
  never whitened by pigeons, that head, man,
  there is no head like it in human history,

  there is no highway to Venice.

Blue Dalmatia

I spied a piece of garterbelt on the stone floor
    near the confessional in St. Marc's,
wonderful Byzantine gold has to be peeling
    as the floor leans and sinks in all directions.

Venice is falling into the sea
    and the church is leading the way.

Now look at these bums on bicycle seats at highway's edge—
    (Did Louis Dudek notice such things?)
The bicycle seat and the bumpy road forgive the church's
    repression of girlhood sex. Maybe the church
has money in the bicycle companies.

    We drove right through Trieste, past its
Okanagan bikinis, and climbed into Yugoslavia, two
    New World gents in a Kraut car. Under a
portrait of Tito we got a great hullabaloo satisfactory
    smear on our passports, a double fistful of frail currency.

Coasting

As you travel Dalmatia southward
      the donkeys, loaded with sticks and peasant women,
appear to have eaten every bit of green
      among the white rocks, the blue
Adriatic far below the only rumoured moisture.

How strange in this conquered country devoid of neon,
      an Australian and a Canadian
in a German auto in Yugoslavia, smoking
      English cigarettes bought on a Belgian ship.

Along the road little girls hold up turtles for sale,
      everything so strange here round the world's other side,
it's all Roman, 100 BC, up to date Socialist,
      the teenage girls unashamed to look innocent,
they have the most open faces of young people anywhere,
      not hounded by fashion magazines and eye makeup.

The Russian magazines have it right.

"Where are we?" asked one of the German tourists.
"Split," I advised.

The spy city

In all these towns people walk the middle of the street
and cars such as ours make their way among them.
I like olden days socialism more and more.

        Skeletal Romans stand in underwater valleys,
        blue Adriatic mountain top islands
        elude all politics, all conquerors.
        There's a swimsuit in my pack, I thought.

The hillsides are full of bullets, but yellow broom
shines below the cypresses, scents our open windows,
road signs sprout Cyrillic words, then here's
        one palm tree,
        one Orthodox dome,
        one Dubrovnik,
        one drawbridge,
        no automobiles, no scooters, no bikes,
        maybe some Shakespeare.

And on Mt. Sergio looking down, the thin fierce
Montenegro people, hawks, standing high,
straight noses, high cheekbones, black hair, piercing black eyes.

Innocent and deadly, ancient and quiet.

A VW cabin in the sky

Those Albanian mountains must be fair
      swarming with soldiers. Skulk and tread
the goat trails, shivering in turned up collars.
      Come down in the valley and have some
Turkish coffee.

          The green Morača River cuts
deep into stratified half-rock, half-soil, slabs
overhanging the water a kilometer below, an illusion,
one of the mist-rivers of child-beloved
fantasy, places that exist, never found.

All the mountain children are so beautiful
      you want to stop and look at them for hours,
they smile and wave, you wave back.

And when we reached Peč for the night
the kids were wearing moccasins with turned-up toes,
women in baggy Moslem pants, tall minarets
in every corner. We have arrived in Arabi.

Prizren

In the town of Prizren
Tony stopped the dusty Volkswagen
and lit out for oranges at a store
while I sat in the car
watching the world go by,
south Yugoslavia,
the strange eastern earth
of veils and yak-drover pantaloons.

I saw a brown wrinkled man
with a baby in his arms,
he's trying his best, crooked legs,
running along the crowded street,
dusty wife following.

The baby's eyes were closed
and his face was bare.
I wondered where
he was going. To the doctor?

How far away?
Is it any use?
Who was I, sitting there
in that strange car
on the side of the powdery street,
the doors locked for safety?

Down Greece

In the customs house, in the bank, at the tollbooth,
the clerks sat at desks crammed together,
stamping papers wildly, shouting across the room,
angrily waving multi-stamped paper smeared
with squares and circles, accusing ink, ignoring us.

On the streets everyone hacked and spit, three-year-old boys,
ninety-year-old grannies, anytime a square foot of
pavement showed, spit and mark the spot.

There was a path leading away from the road, a sign,
"The Spring of the Muses." Down the path we saw
a guy standing beside a cement mixer.

Tony drove from Thessalonica all the way down,
batting at flies that circled his head. We'd left
the high country of the gods, to enter dark human
land.

      But Athens gleams at night. I felt like dancing,
arms up. But there's no room.

Garlic and marble

It was trying to rain. Athens, said Tony,
       and again he was right, like San Francisco. How
sleep the brave? If God made man in his own
       image, in whose image made He the priest?

Swim the street here, passing Greek islands of incense,
       garlic, perfume, oranges, oleander, animal crap,
diesel oil, candy, human crap—breathe and travel,
       see the muses smile, sniff it up, remember.

The dining room was forever filled with groups
       of grey-haired English and German women.
Here they were, free of men and countries, seeing
       immortality in Hellas before going into
their own.

       They all love
       the young Greek waiters.

The Greek relics

In Hellas, nothing has changed in 2500 years.

The kiosks in Constitution Square offer *Teen Muscles* magazine,
along with chewing gum, worry beads and Henry Miller books.

I was looking at the back of the head of a lovely young
blonde woman from northern Europe. Her shiny face
had been a foot from Poseidon's bronze groin
for fifteen minutes.

                      One was surrounded by marble,
by the centuries of men struggling with their chisels.

But at the rain-threatened Acropolis
    a short and homely Greek guard
        hoiked and spat on the Parthenon floor.

From up there Athens was a wide cluster of white buildings.

Down there again it was a crush of people in black.

Corinth

We passed and passed those gentlest of trees,
the olives, ranging as far into the valleys as we
could see, till they were not separate trees but
an olive-green-grey haze. Then there were the mountains.

At ancient Corinth one little mountain of 500 meters.
Sisyphus worked here, and now I learned to doubt
the separation of myth and history. Atop this mountain
lay the low ruins of a castle—that's only history.

At old town Corinth we ate in a no-translation
restaurant, where the best food in Greece warms in pots
over a wide fire—meatballs with rice and gravy,
spiced macaroni, big fat beans with olive oil. Oh.

We passed under the Lion Gate at tremendous Mycenae,
trying to believe, but I didn't have the right
family background.

Notara Street

Tony stashed his VW and climbed onboard a ship
for the islands, walking with a friendly guy on
whose sleeve was written "Interpretor." It was
impossible to follow his English. Here was Piraeus.

I fell into a class D hotel and looked out my window
at an old stone wall full of holes, and pigeons looking out.
They cooed at me, from cotes made 493 BC,
and so did the women on Notara Street.

None of them looked like Melina Mercouri.
Some of them looked like Anthony Quinn.
The US fleet was in and the New Orleans Bar was open.

So was the West Coast Bar, and that was funny. The whores
yelled, "Hey, come inside," but I skulked by, long-haired
in sneakers, I was not any USAmerican's mother's son.

Never on Sunday

In the fleabag hotel I met the nice fat ugly
cleaning woman, woeful creature, bent to her
task on the stairs, slop pail like a child
beside her,
               tries doggedly all day and night
to fight dirt and stink. Her sponge is covered
with white disinfectant.
                        I see her late night
and in the morning, she's on her fat knees,
suffering black hair hanging over her face.

              In the cubicle I am getting the
real peeling wall Billy Burroughs. Ceiling smells
of Mediterranean wine, flush doesn't work. I
have decided I have to do the standing part,
but I won't sit down till we are in our
next town—
              half a weekend to go.

North to Kavala

We passed old Mount Olympus again, rock
covered with clinging rainclouds, sunshine drifting,
god country, I guessed. But no Zeus is good Zeus.

Bright Gypsies with shuffling bears tinkled by.
"I sense the approach of the mystic East," said Tony.
"The scent of cinnamon and rose petals," he said.
"The scent of running sewers and rotting meat."
"The thin, faint sound of little golden bells
                        on a thousand dancing feet," he said,
driving carefully around chickens.
"The thin, faint sound of oxen shit hitting the pavement."
                I pointed out.

But then in that green panhandle northeast,
I learned to love Greece. This was where all
the beautiful Greeks lived!

.

That remote peace—I didn't know that was what
I was looking for. It was the evening of June 6.

Peace on one side of Europe.

Turkey

The last wrist of Greece,
but men have fezes on their knobby heads.

Storks stand atop telegraph poles,
         walk with bony elbows in the marsh.
Women's eyes look over the tops of veils,
         tiny schoolgirls blow pink bubblegum.

. . .

The first dry corner of Turkey,
         a boy was riding a solitary camel.
I expected Cornel Wilde at the sound of a gong.

. . .

In Istanbul at last, look in any direction,
         perne in a gyre, see a spire.
City's full of international hipsters,
         beards and sandals, sheepskin vests,

robbing my adventure.

Even all the Turks at night were Beat Generation characters—
straight out of Burroughs. Dark stares, sallow cheeks,
shuffling moustaches, secret agonized poems
between shoe and sole of foot. Everyone was up
to no good in the dark winding streets of Stamboul.
Black market broken stones, old ruins,
you want a ruin, centuries old?
Hire a wheelbarrow.

Ataturk's bridge

Men trod the streets with huge baskets
       hanging from a rod across the shoulders
              and in the baskets great piles of
strawberries.

Red Istanbul. But in the Topkapi Palace
       USAmericans flashed their cameras, took home
              reflections of flashbulbs off glass cases.

Gold Istanbul. But in the six-minaret mosque
       we walked in sock feet, (my big toe sticking out)
              across acres of carpet, under a far dome

built when Shakespeare went bald. Blue Istanbul.

Attar of roses

In Thracian Turkey huge mosques dominate towns
where men with no legs push along in low carts,
bent people in black hobble through dust,
by rust, skinny old women dig in garbage heaps,
but children dance under the sun
around an old man asleep on a chair, white of hair,
in a white dusty place beside the cobbled road.

. . .

In Thracian Bulgaria the towns are gardens,
streets filled with roses.
Between towns picturesque Slav women
work in Balkan fields, sunflowers to the horizon,
grapes, cabbages, wheat, roses, it is, I said,
stunning. More stunning than the posters
of picturesque women working in fields.

Soldiers play accordions.
Our hotel room was full of roses.
Marlene Dietrich's voice came through the window.
We vowed to live out our lives in Plovdiv.

Wisdom, finally

Down the wide empty streets of Sofia,
beauty, not wisdom, ghosts of people walked
arm in arm under sidewalk trees,
and the present corporeal people walked with them
arm in arm.

Down an industrial canyon of railroad and electricity
we drove to the west,
      into Serbia, to the
Tower of Skulls, mortar and 952 young Serbian heads
piled by a Turkish general, a warning
we knew enough to heed.

Parked in a blind Volkswagen beside the Belgrade road,
we couldn't see out the windshield in the black Newlove rain,
lightning stepping on Highway One,
hail smashing our tin top.
      We smelled the air's
metal burnt by electricity.
       Then we sit, terrified by trucks,
maddened by stones on the roof,
somewhere in the middle of Tito's
beautiful invisible land.

Some Answers

June

Thomas Grey

"Can storied urn or animated bust
 Back to its mansion call the fleeting breath?"

Air goes out more or less forever, yet
 another gust arrives. I can see, though,

why you'd make such inquiry in a graveyard,
 surrounded by marble and concrete, dead

as a doornail. But think positively—you'd
 go on for eighty-six more lines, a lot

of breath in my opinion, doubly so
 for a youth that Melancholy marked for her own.

Christina G. Rossetti

"Who has seen the wind?"

Not, I, but her dance partners,
yes, that swaying willow, that

white plastic grocery bag
among the high wires, another

gust arrives, and we hear it;
if it comes off the sea

we smell it. If we don't
know the dancer from the dance

we think we see it.

William Blake

"Did he who made the lamb make thee?"

The same breath of spring's being
entered us and separated us

till we stood amazed, looking about,
looking to see who started all this,

finally aware only of the need to move,
to take this forest as dance partner,

to cool the fire in each brain,
to look for one another once again.

Henry Wadsworth Longfellow

*"For who has sight so keen and strong
That it can follow the flight of song?"*

Actually, Hank, I use my old ears
to follow the flight of song. I

save my eyes for seeing the wind.
Breathe music as much as you like,

Hank, you still ought to pick up
the accordion, people will love you,

honest. They'll start shouting arrows
into the air, wondering
where they'll fall.

John Dryden

*"What human Voice can reach
The sacred Organ's praise?"*

   The accordion, John, though never
sacred, lies before interior organs

   responsible for notes that wing
their heavenly ways, before they fall

   God knows where. The squeeze box
offers unstinting praise, rowdy

   though it be. Lend an ear to this
lion of song. Who made him made

   the lamb; who loves the lamb
sings with human diaphragm.

William Wordsworth

"Is it a reed that's shaken by the wind,
Or what is it that ye go forth to see?"

We venture there to watch the power
of air, breathed by some hidden chest

and loosed in Nature's tidiest ways,
to bend a reed or ilk a willow.

An oboe was a branch of life
before the artist touched his knife

to shape it to his thought. And yet
the wind that courses through is not

the player's will, but something we
today do rouse ourselves to see.

D. H. Lawrence

"Have you built your ship of death, O have you?"

Ah, Herbie, it's nearly there, afloat in fancy,
seaworthy as any scribbler's page, noble

in silhouette before a Pacific sundown, wet
as wisdom will permit. I am no sailor, yet

I'll practise my knots, trim my sail, punctuate
every sentence of every chapter with home port

in mind. He who made the lamb made the sea
regardless of you and me, our desire

to see the wind before we die.

William Shakespeare

"*But wherefore do not you a mightier way*
Make war upon this bloody tyrant Time?"

Oh, Will, what way is mightier than verse
that luckily survives four hundred years,

what achievement more vain,
I mean—what would you revise today?

Forgive my question. It's your question stirs
my peaceful body to seek a safer hiding place.

I'll elude Time, that son of a bitch, I'll
ensconce myself behind a wall of prose, I'll

whisper your name in twenty-first century
English, I'll rise against any tyrant

but this bastard. I'll slide in and
become him, I'll
haul you from your place,
I'll bring you past Eternity.

Charles Olson

*"What soul
is without fault?"*

I once aimed for that, to be
blameless, monstrously,
        some will have it,
purely, I thought why not, given
one whole life?

        This before
they introduced the notion of
inherited sin, or sinfulness, or
maybe after.

        I never made it, though
I gave myself a chance, the chance
to say
        this one, sir, this one
        in any case.

Walt Whitman

*"Have you no thought O dreamer
 that it may be all maya, illusion?"*

I always say why think about such a thing.
If it's all maya, then let me take part in maya.
If I drop a cannon ball on a glacier's smooth expanse.
I don't care whether it's illusion,
and if red poppies spring from the black in white
you won't hear me claiming they are real.

Yes, if I am your dreamer, Walt,
 I'll dream your question away.
I'll lie between you and your maya
 and fondle you both.

Thomas Hardy

"Who thinketh no evil, but sings?
Who is divine?"

                              I am too
modest to raise my wing,

void of hope along with anger,
I blush despite an aged skin.

Yet I recall my vow when ten
to think no evil,
                barely able to
                carry a tune,

I gave no thought to godliness
but only to express the wind
in my heart,
                to convert the silver
pin affixèd there.

T. S. Eliot

"Shall I part my hair behind?"

Well, just about everyone's behind
is parted.

If you have a hair behind, though,
you might think about a depilatory
or a wax job.

Especially if you expect
any kind of sex life. The mermaids,
for example, combing
the white hair of the waves,

perhaps parting it. Such sweet
sorrow. No, don't part it,
shave it, then
shove it.

Alexander Pope

*"Who to a friend his faults can freely show,
And gladly praise the merit of a foe?"*

I do confess it difficult to do,
though promising to start today at two.

My faults are very small, so hard to see,
and merits in my foes so much like me.

How sad, my oldest friend has lost his sight,
and none among my foes is fit to fight.

I'll love my foe, I'll hate my several sins,
when all the fish have feathers, birds have fins.

Helen Adam

"Can no man ever escape from love
    who breaks from a woman's womb?"

Not a chinaberry's chance; love
    will climb from the grave to get him.

Love will ride the wind unseen
    and the air will close behind her.

As a fish through the sea, as an
    arrow through air, love

leaves no trail, pain
    was gathered by the mother in question.

In her pain she smiled.
    thinking that was her only love

she saw pursuing her bairn.

Louis Dudek

"What kind of honey
    does a bee get from a thistle?"

Baptist honey, puritan honey, work
    for your living honey, the kind
of poem you pull on and bend back and forth
    till it gives you your aha!

Honey is not blood, it doesn't
    come easy, it is sweeter than
perspiration, but you have to sweat
    in a country of thistles, the country

you ought to choose. I mean if your mother
    didn't spoil you. And Louis?
I know you knew this all along,
    tall Montreal brother lying down at last.

Percy Bysshe Shelley

*"What thou art we know not;
    What is most like thee?"*

Were I a skylark, not a poet,
    I might sing your answer,

harmonious madness from deep
    in your own brain.

Where you thinketh no evil,
    but dream the rise of those

grey-brown, divine, hungry, sick,
    prisoners of habit, subjects

of oil millionaires locked inside
    their own election prisons.

Thy mind Alastor is most like,
    thy song insane and lovely.

H.D.

*"Why wait for Death to sow
us in the ground?"*

Ah, an old woman
asks an old man
an agricultural question

who left his native
farming country as a young
admirer of the apple tree, the pear

you loved too. I'm avoiding
not the question but the answer,
thus making verse

from the brown leaves
we're surprised to see
at our extremities.

Sylvia Plath

*"Is it the sea you hear in me,
Its dissatisfactions?"*

Ah, no, not the sea in your roots
but the wind in your branches,
nicht wahr?

       Or your branches
thrust into the wind no one
else sees. You are so
Aeolian, you sing so well

your self, your own
dissatisfactions.

         If winter comes
you will notice in lovely music
its effect on you.

Paul Valéry

*"Qui pleure là, sinon le vent simple, à cette heure
Seule, avec diamants extremes?"*

Not I, but the wind, I am tempted to say,
the selfsame breath of autumn's being
come to visit us in June, out of season
my poor heart, wishing this were all maya.

Who weeps indeed, who mourns cock robin,
neither you nor I. It is your heart's poem, Pablo,
it is your small sweet word in the eternal anthology,
your throw across this beautiful ultimate diamond.

Who is divine? What is most like thee? Sing,
earthly muse, sound the loneliness right out
of this hour.

John Donne

"Must business thee from hence remove?"

Not business, but love, for you are business
and she is away.
                   I mean your maddening
beautiful verses became in late time
a means to earn my paycheque, hone my brain
for more.
            But she never recites a quatrain,
nor bends a word to its own surcease. She
simply loves my simple sentence
because it says I need her.

Phyllis Webb

"*Was it only
last night?*"

No, it was
eternity.

Yes, time is an
arrow, you quiver.

You trembled
last night, miss.

I saw eternity
the other night.

It was first
night, too, first.

Yes, last night it
was definitely only.

John Keats

"What is more gentle than a wind in summer?"

But consider whence it came
        and where it goes now, consider
the summer being
        of whom it is a breath. I know
you hear an alluring rime there
        and who's to blame you? You
do not want to wait and hear
        the news in winter's gale. You
feel that breeze on your uncovered cheek,
        you care not for its language, you
are a set of strings. But list
        for just the length of a heart-beat.

It touches you gently, but it speaks
        a message only poesie can pass.

Sappho

"To what, O beloved bridegroom,
 may I compare you?"

If you suggest a summer's day
I'll walk off this island.

If you suggest a former husband
I can't say I'll try my best.

I don't know whether
I'm in favour of a simile at all.

How about some more adventurous
figure of speech, dear poet wife.

I recommend antiphrasis,
as in calling me "beloved bridegroom."

William Carlos Williams

*"A quatrain? Is that
the end I envision?"*

Or are you lost, having
thought of an end?

A waking dream starts
you off just as well,
no question about it.
See what you see,

hear what you hear,
imagine punctuating
a gift fallen into
your half-awake lap.

You are found every time,
not knowing the power
of your words to keep
the end out of sight.

Lorine Niedecker

"Can knowledge be conveyed that isn't felt?"

I've heard your answer to that
      in your clear-spoken poems.

I've heard the loud birds over your cabin,
      and seen the fish jumping out of the river.

I don't think I learned anything; I felt
      what I'd call "nice,"

though I'd been puking all day. You
      toiled your whole life in an America

no one imagines. Knowledge is piled
      in city libraries and police stations.

There's a popcorn can lid nailed over a hole
      to keep winter from mousing into your kitchen.

You got that across.

Emily Dickinson

"For what are Stars but Asterisks
 To point a human life?"

Many are huge balls of burning gas
 that care for no person

except Ralph Waldo Emerson, who thinks
 the universe the externization of the soul,

and Samuel Taylor Coleridge, who seeks
 to make the external internal, nature

thought, and maybe Walt Whitman, who
 thinks he is a cosmos himself.

I have no opinion on the matter,
 but I do have to admit that stars

resemble asterisks—that is why
 we start the word with "aster."

William Butler Yeats

"When shall the stars be blown about the sky,
Like the sparks blown out of a smithy, and die?"

Or do they resemble asterisks blown by some wind
out of the human heart onto the very page

you are reading?   *   *   *

                         *

                                    *

                                              *

*

       *   Or dancers—no, we can distinguish
dancers from just about anything, from celestial
punctuation, from questions themselves.

The last time I heard, the smithy was a soul,
and any spark extinguished therefrom
diminishes the continent and the sky over it.

Robert Creeley

"*what groans so pathetically*
in this room where I am alone?"

Not I, but the wind,
the tree rubbing against the roof,

the anxious heart only human
after all, no matter the muse,

no matter your wedding
with the world; the dark fills

the corners of the room, your own
breath whispers the end, the end,

what else was the cosmos made for,
and how long did you think it would last?

Robert Kroetsch

"Does the body teach us nothing?"

Dear Bob:

1. That's for me to know
     and you to find out.

2. Wouldn't *you* like to know?

3. If I told you,
     we'd both know.

4. If I knew,
     I wouldn't tell you.

5. Don't ask *me*.

6. Ask me no questions,
     and I'll tell you no lies.

Besides,
     if you want to learn nothing,
where else would you go?

Ron Padgett

"*How can we arrange everything so that everything is great?*"

Arranging is out of the question;
it's begging the question,
                        begging—I
always say, why think of such a thing,
it may be nothing, the nothing you have learned,
nothing but maya,
                only illusion.
                              Nothing
will be great once we get it,
                    a white
plastic grocery bag filled with nothing, totally
filled.

    I love you, Ron, but I love the wind
your smart brain's voice even more. It can't
be far behind.

Shall I Compare

July

I sit to
        watch your hair
                change its shape

Every morning bright
              coils up top
                        shake down soft

Colours spill what
            are they now
                      oh newborn head

Yes it feels
 like a coconut
  your dear head

I don't climb
 high palms but
  wait for fall

Oh shapely food
 you fancy me
  my own tropic

I have perfect
            ears you say
                        each damn day

I put my
        tongue in one
                    when I can

If you hear
            what I whisper
                        touch me there

There are no
            lips so plush
                        as your two

A hail storm
            in my heart's
                        now a brook

This is what
            they mean by
                        a wet kiss

Eyes like two
              sad question marks
                            in the rain

Drive me to
              make a simile
                            hop the fence

Wink at me
              ah come on
                            just this once

In your sleep
          your Scottish nose
                    is a triangle

I love to
     kiss the top
            wake you up

One two three
         your cool nose
                plans my day

Did he who
         made the Lamb
                  make thy neck

It isn't long
        it isn't narrow
                it isn't cool

To the Lamb
        I say bah
                now let's neck

Your human hand
                nature's most astonishing
                                  living power machine

It's often in
        the hardware shop
                      touching or lifting

I'm a witness
        that lovely power
                holds me up

Your thumbs are
              like your big
                            toes see below

Your fingers say
              monkey texture just
                            exactly like this

Your hand tremor
              makes crossword and
                            me get solved

Today you went
    to buy a
        bra why bother

Lean on me
    face me and
       lean on me

Thinking both thinking
        two thinking you
            in the plural

Your wrists at
              the steering wheel
                            two intelligent twigs

I circle them
          with my fancy
                      on this highway

Round I go
         and where we
                   stop you know

I smell roses
           when your lovely
                      face nears mine

But no such
           roses see I
                    in your cheeks

Flowering is not
           my name nor
                    what we do

Shake a lance
           I will watch
                      your strong arm

Bared you are
           nigh to me
                      in your power

Your biceps will
           bisect my heart
                      trip my verse

I have your
>   heart right hear
>   heat and art

My left fist
>   the same size
>   aye orta know

Eye and ear
>   sense the pounding
>   wake me up

You are singular
            but a pear
                        to be paird

Your back turned
            my sweet bairn
                        I thee wed

I walk behind
            to watch thee
                        sashay thy tread

You smile you
            stick your tongue
                        out at me

Just a suggestion
            you are saying
                        out it comes

I say who's
            writing this poem
                        you or eye?

Expensive spirits bend
                        my head to
                                      your dear waist

'Twould be a
                shame to pursue
                                some madness instead

A bliss in
            forty proof wins
                          our winsome way

Ah your round
            belly will never
                        sag in poetry

This verse'll sound
            as long as
                        men can breathe

And your sweet
            globe will take
                        their breath away

I love to
         feel your hands
                  guiding my head

And in this
         change too is
                  my invention spent

My tongue speaks
         a sentence you
                  delight to rhyme

I'll not say
        nay to navel
                nor anus say

Hooray I may
        find a way
                a path eh

Sym-pathetic you say
        the way you
                pay our way

In the Volvo
  　　　　I spy your
  　　　　　　　　knee and grab

Gently I grab
  　　　　and wonder more
  　　　　　　　　at the pleasure

What makes this
  　　　　measure where does
  　　　　　　　　it come from

Your unstockinged leg
                      leading to the
                                      earth is fine

Behind my ear
              is better enough
                              said about that

Your leg steps
          I follow all
                      the way up

I groan pathetically
                in this room
                              where I'm alone

Your semistockinged thigh
                      is not here
                                  I am alone

I think on
          your naked thigh
                        and I groan

Your feet upon
                which you neglect
                              to wear socks

I can hold
        one in each
                cream covered hand

Only the imagination
                said Dr. Williams
                              only trust that

Blunt thy toe
           blunt this verse
                      grunt my heart

Oh kick me
           not oh buss
                      me wicked one

Oh digits two
           tough flowers of
                      meat I kiss

I placed my
        poet's hand upon
                your scrumptious knee

Your next move
        said you'd not
                read Irving Layton

I'd haply found
        two more reasons
                to adore you

I dreamed this
              mortal part of
                            yours and mine

Was changed into
              a stalk and
                            not a vine

I'll quickly grant
              your taste for
                            gardening is fine

You understand I
           love the lines
                      in your forehead

Wise you are
        immortalized in these
                  lines less dear

My words reach
        toward the music
                of your brow

You are more
            than the sum
                        of your parts

Some of your
            parts too are
                        more than all

You are particularly
            some total I
                        love to enumerate

Not to objectify
············as they say
························your numerous assets

Nor to accentuate
············the trace of
························your country charm

My verses try
············to keep abreast
························of your spirit

Head to toe
          I tell you
                    head to toe

I rub you
          I taste you
                    I love you

This male gaze
              just an old
                        guy's lust hooray

According to Brueghel

August

According to Curnoe
the R34
floated to a piano

accompaniment, the orange
lighter than air
vessel bore on its nose

a French roundel, Peter
with eyeglasses
blew baritone sax

the sixties
meant bright colours
for Greg

as did the seventies
but who is
the guy in the

snap-brim hat
maybe mister
leadfoot

According to Thomson
the sky was
made of coloured bricks

the lake
was the sky
also back of

a ragged northern
jack pine
bricks

separated by
blue hills daubed
with snow, we

always think
there's no people
in his Ontario

but it's full
of humanity
piling bricks

According to Caravaggio
Holofernes woke up
with his head

half off
his eyes and mouth
wide open

Judith rolled
her sleeves up
to reveal muscled arms

but she held
the long sword wrong
so it must

have been sharp
as her nose is
sharp under her frown

his right hand
means he was trying
to rise

According to Krieghoff
when *les habitants* played cards
all the men

wore hats
thirteen French Canadians
crowded one end

of a planked room
dogs here
and there

no one sits
on this side
of the table

as in the Last Supper
only the painter
looks in their direction

that table and those
chairs are now
worth a fortune

According to Brainard
the sky has
ten stars

one crescent moon
a yellow butterfly
and many flowers

some perhaps
in a vase
we see

something torn
and remember
that most of Emerson

heads for a
star if you turn
off the lights

in collage
how is anything
far or near

According to Chagall
it was twenty after seven
when the blue-legged bird man

flew or was it
hopped into view
his eye upside down

a juggler
on his torso
and an eye

inverted on his
head, green above
and red below

the eerie apparition
is quieted
by people surrounding him

mother and children
fading into sight
wings over everything

According to Collier
Lady Godiva
straddled her horse

no stirrups
for her bare feet
her weight what

there was of it
on the high
hard saddle

her lithesome white
body could be
a boy's

or a hipless girl's
her head looking down
in modesty

not like your
usual social
activist noble woman

According to Cézanne
it was about
all he could do

for the swan
to lift Leda's
right wrist

that is the swan's
neck at least
is thin

poor cob
and she of some
girth, awaiting perhaps

a sudden blow:
I think that
bird god

had better
count his feathers
before loosing anything

According to Poussin
when baby Moses was saved
there were a dozen witnesses

a big naked guy
clutched a vase
filled with flowers

all the women
had fair skin
and bare arms

there were narrow
pyramids around town
and a person

imitating the sphinx
nearby men dancing
or fighting barefoot

on the dark river
a boat full of people
is coming or going

According to van Dyck
Cupid and Psyche
had coloured sheets

trailing across
their sexual parts
his red

hers blue
where she reclined naked
against a jutting rock

he ran toward her
reaching as if
to grab something

he had little wings
for decoration
one assumes

I mean
what creature
has arms *and* wings?

According to Modigliani
Diego Rivera
was Buddha

round as Gertrude
Stein, blue
of face and shirt

unlike Amedeo's women
he has no neck
and wide face

Diego has a tuft
of hair on his chin
and more on his head

he is in repose
not stiff as in
photos, settled

a girth for
an Asian world
here in France

According to David
Cupid was a
smirking teenager

with a tan
beside the white
chicken Psyche

his bow
leans on their couch
under his leg

his arrow you
might say is covered
by red cloth

her elbow
rests upon it
and though

her eyes are closed
there is a trace of
smile on her lips

According to Rivera
the children
do not smile

their black hair
hangs over their
foreheads, scissored

their eyes are
huge and black
as their trousers

are white, no
questions asked
one carries his wide hat

above his bare
brown feet, and
the other has

bare feet too
they are México
and what awaits

According to Manet
artists leave
their clothes on

even their cravats
while having breakfast
on the grass

the young women
are models, they're
easy with their skin

it was a sunny
day in the French
woods

darkness fell
from the Italian sky
for Georgione's nymphs

bright skin at their
fête with the
shadowed male musicians

According to Morrisseau
the Thunderbird
is covered

with eyes
or he is filled
with eyes

the lunar spirit
alert inside
his chest

the Thunderbird
is every colour
nature can make

Anishinabe
breath can imagine
rapt artist

can keep apace of
how wide awake
that bird must be

According to Michelangelo
when God touched fingers
with Adam

the latter
was naked
and muscular

while his Creator
was wrapped
in a see-through shift

nine naked figures
held God under
a flying blanket

while his creation
lolled on a
steep tree

but mainly it's
their faces, looking
with that manly love

According to Michelangelo
when Jesus died
his mother was nineteen

he was a thin
marble boy
across her lap

her hand
in his armpit
was larger than her face

his hands
and feet
were unmarked

they were one
piece of white
stone, smooth,

siblings, young
while the world
grew old

According to Michelangelo
Moses had
yes, everyone knows

the story, but look
how realistic
the thin tablets

the nose
that lets you know
this was someone

in Italy
not the Sinai
a place to sit

with loveable
muscular arms, with
knuckles you know

not a father
maybe, but a
splendid scary uncle

According to
the Etruscan sculptor
the magnate

thought he was
above it all
in his tomb

Tarquínia
was as high
as it gets

and lying on top
of a classy
sarcophagus

with hands
used to holding things
carefully wrought

must show power
even when no one knows
who you are

According to Donatello
the Baptist wore
nothing under his

hairy cloak. His naked
leg and side
show none of

that Michelangelo brawn
but a tired man's
servant shapeliness

his teeth too
are even
visible though

he does not smile
he carries paper
and a small

cross, images
of prophecy, meaning
of his name

According to Giotto
when St. Francis died
the monks

could not contain
themselves, they
buried their

faces, they kissed
his feet, they
were overdressed

like the dying
man himself
overdressed, they

were hot brothers
kneeling and
standing, there was

not an animal
in sight, no women
and no animals

According to Leonardo
when the angel
told Mary she was pregnant

she lived in
central Italy
and she was a blonde

her chubby cheeks
white, her curled hair
yellow, her eyebrows

just about
gone, groomed as the
trees outside

her palace. Jesus
would learn the language
of the Medicis

and the superior
sense of design
their angel passed on

According to Tintoretto
the disciples
at the Last Supper

sat both
sides of the table
while Jesus

seemed to be putting
something to eat
into Peter's mouth

nearby a tot
sucked at his
mother's teat, up above

humanoid figures in robes
watched waiters bringing
more edibles

and behind all
an orange hole in the sky
made the lamp unnecessary

According to "Leonardo"
the swan
ugly as he was

didn't have a chance
much as he
wanted her

she had eyes only
for the four
fat babies

broken from their
swan eggs, no
Leda eggs

with his wing
around her ass
and disfiguring longing

in his face
he doesn't see that not
one hair on her head is out of place

According to il
Beato Angelico, Mary
and the angel

were both
a little chilly, though
maybe they were simply

miming rocking a
bambino, the angel
not much more than

a child himself
there on the loggia
where the two blonds

angel and woman
wear haloes dull
compared to his rainbow

wings, and outside
the high fence
nature looks warm enough

According to Botticelli
when the angel
brought Mary the news

there was a terrific
breeze, Mary
was holding an imaginary

baby, the angel was
hovering with
wings up and wrists

crossed, a kind of
hint, perhaps
that life would

not always be
this costly palace
of silk beds

or the weather
calm and the hills
topped with three trees

According to Martini
Mary was a little annoyed
when the angel

dropped by, her thumb
holding her place
in the book

she was reading, a
Gutenberg in red
binding, her mouth

turned down, her
head turned away
but the angel

with leaves on
his head, a sprig
in his hand

sent his movable golden
letters to her turned
not right now ear

According to Holliday
when Dante met Beatrice
it was right in front

of our hotel. Remember
who Jean was almost
at the end of *Baseball*

Love, here the sponda
wind blew the thin
cloth against her legs

and who then
thought of a paradiso
spiritual? Was Dante

holding his heart
or posing with his
costly raiment? Those

flimsy shoes
would never get
anyone through hell

According to Caravaggio
teenaged Saint
John the Baptist

was a naked
swastika, so open
to gaze

he seems open
to hands, desirable
even to those who

do not so
desire, Caravaggio
had his light side

and, one supposes, oh
what stuffy
language, some sort of

Christianity that might ask
who took those clothes
off young John—himself?

According to Bassano
at the Last Supper
everyone was drunk

sprawling on
the tablecloth, gesturing
manically, the

disciples shouting
at one another
standing and falling

all except Jesus
who stood
behind the youngest

a cross-shaped halo
behind his head
thinking of his ordeal

that these bearded
gesticulating men
could not face

According to Sodoma
Mary was no kid
when she held the

slain Jesus, mostly
in darkness, the
darkness around his face

and her face
a worn light
in darkness, her hands

held his shoulder
and his knee, his
hands useless

but there was a wan
light beyond the hill
where trees, not crosses

stood back against
a sky that seemed
nowhere, no place for a mother

Fulgencio

September

Hatuey would not tell the Spanish
where the gold was.

                  On February 15, 1512
they tied him to a post. The priest
advised conversion to Christianity, the sole way
to reach Heaven.

                  Are you Christians, Hatuey asked,
going to Heaven? Yes, said the priest, if we
die in the Grace of God.

                  Then I won't go,
said Hatuey. I don't want to see
any more Christians.

                  So the priest
and his armed Spaniards burnt the Cuban man
and went looking
                  for someone else
to find their gold for the stately churches
of whitened Europe.

If we seize Cuba, said Thomas Jefferson,
the Architect of Democracy,
we will be masters of the Caribbean.

Teddy Roosevelt kept quiet and carried
a big stick to San Juan Hill, leading
his 6,000 Rough Riders against
700 Spanish defenders. 102 Spanish died,
along with 223 invaders. Teddy
became famous and president, just like
the Architect of Democracy.

There will be some forty to fifty
great States, wrote Walt Whitman, Poet
of Democracy, among them Canada and Cuba.

President Howard Taft agreed. The whole
hemisphere, he said, will be ours in fact as,
by virtue of our superiority of race,
it already is ours morally.

January 1, 1899,
sixty years to the day before the Fidelistas
entered la Habana,
                    the Spanish flag
was lowered, the U.S. flag raised.

    After years of impatience, the Yanks
now owned their biggest island.
        The Cubans who had fought the Spanish
all these years
            were not invited to the show.
Too many of them were black.

        The U.S. officers liked the Spaniards
better than these dark revolutionaries.
        War correspondent Winston Churchill
said we cannot have another island
run by those Africans.

Two years and two weeks later
Fulgencio Batista y Zaldívar
was born where Columbus had landed,
born out of every poor Cuban's blood.

1903, the Platt Amendment pronounced
"that all Acts of the United States in Cuba
during its military occupancy thereof are
ratified and validated, and all
lawful rights acquired thereunder
shall be maintained and protected."

                     By troops and ships,
by white Yankees and
the natural course of history. Wasn't
that proclaimed by James
Monroe?

                     Fulgencio was nearly two.
If you looked at him kind of sideways
he might have been a little Filipino or
Indio, a little African, Spanish, which
was African enough, don't you think?

Young Fulgencio observed
    la Regla de Ocha, he
eyed Elegba, he was a poor boy
interested in gates and roads, like
Saint Antony, Elegba's slave name.

    He liked drums, not books,
    he wanted an Orisha in his chest,
    he didn't mind offering some chicken blood.

But the new owners
    had a worship called sugar.
La Regla went into the forest
    while the canes
    were taken by Coca Cola,
    by Hershey,
    their steel rails
    where the holy way used to be.

Young Fulgencio put sugar
    into his coffee.

When Menocal, the U.S. favourite,
won re-election in 1916, there were
more votes cast than there were
eligible voters.

    Real currency paid for
imaginary roads. Real U.S. Marines
stayed till 1923.

     Real U.S. cabinet members
and mill-owners imported real U.S.
attitudes toward Africans in the new world.

Cuba became a playground
for USAmericans who could afford
to sail away
    from Prohibition.

In 1921 Fulgencio Batista joined the army.

Everyone hated Gerardo Machado
except for Calvin Coolidge. Coolidge
got Machado elected in 1928,

admired the way Machado handled
labour union leaders in the Depression,
throwing them to real sharks offshore.

Now the army kept Machado in power
till Franklin Delano Roosevelt came along.
This Roosevelt wanted his own puppet.

Machado left for Nassau with
seven bags of gold. Roosevelt got Céspedes,
but everyone else hated Carlos Manuel de Céspedes.

When I was a boy with books
I yearned for "America," though I
wondered why they were so late
getting into fights with Hitler and Tojo.

Justice, I knew, created the United States,
freedom and justice, the Lone Ranger
and Superman, sidekicks of colour
who only said "Ugh!" but loved justice.

Sergeant Fulgencio Batista grabbed the army,
joined the students, fired some white officers
and relieved Céspedes of his power.
Mulatto Batista gave it to Professor Grau,

and FDR's friend Sumner Welles, named
after a famous abolitionist, called the ruling group
"frankly communistic." He started seeing
the recently retired white officers.

The yanquis didn't like Professor Grau.
He dumped the U.S.-made constitution.
He started the eight-hour work day.
He took over the U.S.-owned electric company.
He gave jobs to Cubans.
He let the Cuban women vote.
He legalized maternity leave for workers
and child care for infants.

U.S. Ambassador Welles told his president
not to recognize Professor Grau's government.

Then he went to talk to Sergeant Batista.

Batista was kind of dark-skinned.
His grandpa was Chinese and all.
But what could you do?
He could manage, you know, stability.

Batista became a colonel and
Chief of Staff. They liked him more and more
in Washington. In the middle of the Depression
he talked to Professor Grau. In January

Batista handed over a new figurehead
and in five days
Washington recognized him.

The Land of the Free
took an easy breath.
The sharks in Havana's bay
recognized the new government too.

Today is September 11th.
We Americans remember this date.
It's the date upon which the CIA
machine-gunned the elected president of Chile.
11/9 we've called it ever since.

We were a little shocked.
Chile was a rare democracy and all.
And machine guns?
The CIA didn't machine-gun
the elected president of Guatemala.
They only had to point machine guns at him.

Back in 1940 Fulgencio Batista
became president of Cuba
with a new
constitution. It made the U.S. president
uneasy. It included a minimum wage.

President Batista joined the war against tyranny,
1941–1944, signed nine military agreements
with the U.S. armed forces, said
come on in, *mi casa es su casa*,
let's fight fascism,
got richer and richer.

the pretty mulatto handed government,
man by man, back to the civilians,
handed the economy to the yanquis,
retired in 1944, gold dust in his hair,
to a Florida mansion near his pal,
Meyer Lansky.

        Mr. Lansky went to school
with Lucky Luciano and Bugsy Siegel.

In 1941–1944, Meyer and Bugsy were patriotic
eyes for the U.S. Office of Naval Intelligence.

But he was back in 1952,
back with a *golpe*, he and his army
seized, as we heard once in a while,
power.

>Threw out the Congress,
>wrote a new constitution,
>this army clerk,
>banned political parties,

>put out his hand
>to the bankers, the landowners,
>the sugar kings, the *industrialistos*.

It took seventeen days
>for the U.S. to recognize his rule.

The Catholic church and U.S. Steel
>dittoed that.

>Eisenhower smiled like a granddad.

U.S. Ambassador to Cuba Arthur Gardner said
"Batista had always leaned toward the United States.
I don't think we ever had a better friend.
…
It was regrettable that he was known
to be getting a cut."

In 1954 Fulgencio stepped down as *caudillo*
and won an election
against nobody.

Vice President Richard Nixon came calling.
He gave the new president a U.S. Medal of Honor
and called him Cuba's Abraham Lincoln.

Meyer Lansky voted Republican.

The Orisha and the army
told *el Presidente* he was invaluable.
So he declared a general amnesty,
and on May 15, 1955, Fidel and Raúl
got out of jail alive.

Robin Hood and his merry men
took to the hills. Daughters of rich Cubans
threw away their high heels
              and became Fidelistas.
Celia, Haydée and Vilma
celebrated July 26.

The heroes appeared in New York newspapers
and French journals.
All Batista had left
was the army, oh, and U.S. businessmen,
and the Mafia, and, well, the
U.S. government.

In 1956 Batista was made
              an honorary citizen of Texas.

Happy New Year!
2:00 a.m., January 1, 1959

Fulgencio and his friends left the island
bound for Santo Domingo,

carrying a lot of personal riches
Nixon's friend Rebozo's friend Lansky
would forward safely to Switzerland
after the usual commission.

Nixon wasn't looking, he was busy
gearing up to be president,
intent on his own fortune.

That day Santiago said ¡*Buenos Dias!* to Fidel.
La Habana said ¡*Hola!* to Che and Camilo.

Nobody remembered the Maine.

I'll tell you something—
in 1958 I wouldn't have had
Fulgencio Batista on my
fantasy civil war team.

He was over the hill.
It had been six years since he'd beaten
Fidel Castro and the Orthodox Party
with a nifty pre-election *golpe*.

Chased those *barbudos*
    into the hills.
Sent croupier scrapings
    into the Alps.

Shook Frank Sinatra's hand.

Joe "Bananas" Bonnano died a millionaire at 97.
Frank Costello died in his sleep at 82.
Vito Genovese died in prison at 72.
Albert Anastasia was filled with lead in a barber's chair at 54.
Tommy Lucchese died of a brain tumour at 68.
    Politicians and judges came to his funeral.
Joe Adonis died during a police interrogation in Rome, at 70.
Santos Trafficante Jr. died after heart surgery in Houston, at 73.
Lucky Luciano, *il capo di tutti capi* dropped dead
    on a Naples runway at 66.

But for a week in February, 1947
    they were guests of Meyer Lansky in Havana.

He got Ol' Blue Eyes to sing to them.
He passed the fedora and raised walking around money
    for Fulgencio Batista,
        who didn't even speak Italian.

Lansky and Batista,
                      what an outfit!
In the 1950s their hotels
        sprang up on the waterfront.
They were, as they say in the roulette biz
        "raking it in."

In 1948 Dewey was supposed to win
        and the mob was supposed to
                govern the U.S. of America.

But things worked out, ¿verdad?
        Batista paid Lansky $25,000 a year
to keep out the crooked games.
        Lansky was to business reform
as Batista was to democracy.

The United Fruit Company
                rolled the dice.

Batista's bombers landed and refueled at Guantánamo;
wasn't he lucky that the United States had
lots of bombs there to lend to the Cuban government?
It was an emergency, so what
if the Guantánamo lease prohibited such a deal?

Fifty years later we wonder
how the world put up with it—
the United States, bulwark of freedom
breaking the terms of the Guantánamo lease?

Eh?

"*Yo soy un hombre sincero.*"

You have to give him that.

The word came from Washington:
create two, three … many Batistas.
Create Diem, Trujillo, Saddam Hussein,
create Noriega, Bin Laden, Somoza,
create Pinochet, Galtieri, Ríos Montt,
create Torrijos, Viola, Stroessner,
create Duvalier and son.

School them at Ft. Benning, Georgia.
Change the name from School of the Americas to
the Western Hemisphere Institute for Security Cooperation.
Tip your forage cap to George Orwell.
Give courses on torture, assassination,
dictatorship and dollars.

This is called the Monroe Doctrine.
This is sometimes called Manifest Destiny.
Other times it is called the Good Neighbor Policy.

We know it as Coca-Cola.

Every time you peeled a Chiquita banana
you voted for the CIA.
Or to put it in a less inflammatory way,
here's a shortened list of United Fruit Company
executives:
>	John Foster Dulles,
>	Allen W. Dulles,
>	Henry Cabot Lodge,
>	Satan.

A couple of those fellows,
brothers, in fact,
got paid by the Schroeder Bank.

The Schroeder Bank was Hitler's financial arm.
The Schroeder Bank was partnered with
>	(surprise ...)
>	the United Fruit Company.

Allen Dulles was CIA director in 1954
>	when United Fruit
>	overthrew the government of Guatemala.

Batista left town with 40 million
>	dollars to peel.

Arthur Schlesinger Jr. said to Louis A. Perez:

> "My fellow countrymen
> reeled through the streets,
> picking up fourteen-year-old Cuban girls
> and tossing coins to make men scramble in the gutter.
>
> One wondered how any Cuban
> could regard the United States with anything
> but hatred."

Meyer Lansky said to Lucky Luciano:

> "We don't want war or revolution here.
> All we need is peace,
> so that we can get on with the business."

John F. Kennedy told the *New York Times*:

> "We hailed Batista
> at a time when Batista
> was murdering thousands."

From their flower-bordered rental
                on the Portuguese shore
the Batistas sometimes motored across Spain
or visited their four schoolboy sons in Switzerland,
where most of their money was.

He wrote book after book,
                earning calluses on his fingers.

There were other unemployed dictators in Estoril,
and an active one across town.

The social life in Lisbon
                was made to order for this
                Spanish, African, Filipino
                writer of memoirs
                in his sweat suit
                and horned-rim glasses.

"I fear too much enthusiasm for Russia,"
    said civilian Batista y Zaldívar.

"If the Russians are given their way
    in any part of the world,
    they will end up owning all of it anyway."

He would rather have been living in Florida again.
    Three of his many children,
    one of his brothers,
    and his former wife
    all lived in Miami.

He managed to save a lot of money
    while he was employed in Cuba.
    Why wouldn't the yanquis
    let him spend it at a racetrack
    in Florida?

Fulgencio's grandson Raoul Cantero III
was Governor Jeb Bush's first appointment
to the Florida Supreme Court.

                        Is it
too sickening to go on? Raoul Cantero II
served under Batista in his secret
"anti-communist" police, refining
torture and assassination. Now he's a nice dad
with a white moustache in Miami.

Remember Orlando Bosch? He's the terrorist
who bazooka'd a Polish freighter in Miami.
Then he blew up an Air Cubana passenger plane
off Barbados, killing Guyanese students
and young Caribbean fencers.

He kept breaking parole
till Jeb Bush's dad said, ah, set him free.
His lawyer was Raoul Cantero III. Raoul
called Orlando a Cuban patriot.

Remember, Richard Nixon called Raoul's grandpa
a Cuban Abraham Lincoln.
Nixon didn't go to jail, either.

Ex-Cuban,
would-be-USAmerican
Fulgencio Batista
died in Spain
seventy-five years after Cuba
      won independence from Spain,
and Fulgencio Batista
died in luxurious Guadalamina, Spain,
being forbidden to return to Florida,
fourteen years after Cuba
      won independence from the USA.

Nowadays,
if you want to stay and golf in Guadalamina,
it'll set you back 2,500 Euros a week.

Going to church is free
except in the tourist season,
and you might see on the church wall
some beaten gold that used to be
in the earth of the New World.

Miami University has two things:
a successful football team
with incomprehensible logo on its helmets,
and the papers
of Fulgencio Batista,
grandfather of onetime football player
Raoul Cantero III, the only member of
    the Florida Supreme Court
to get there without ever being a judge.

Well, his granddad got to be general
without ever being a lieutenant,
and "Cuba's Abraham Lincoln"
without ever freeing a slave.

The bad neighbor policy persists.
But when a hurricane demolished black New Orleans
and the U.S. president was preoccupied elsewhere,
the Cuban president offered doctors and nurses
and blankets and medicine and sweet socialist faces,
the U.S. president didn't reply,
and when the Cuban president said
we'll pay for everything, all our travel,
all our housing, the U.S. president
was photographed looking out a window
high above flooded African American New Orleans.

The Cubans have more doctors per capita
than anyone else. It wasn't as if
they couldn't afford the free house call.

Free health care,
free medicine,
free hospital,
free nursing home,
free child care,
free university,
and the lowest infant mortality rate in the world

started happening when Meyer Lansky,
Fulgencio Batista, and
Uncle Sam
left the island.

Except for Guantánamo.

Tocking Heads

October

With thanks to:

San Francisco Chronicle
Vancouver Sun
Toronto *Globe & Mail*
Toronto Star
Niagara This Week
Welland Tribune
Metro Vancouver
Victoria *Times Colonist*

Red West Shifting to Blue

Communist Montana,
       Socialist Wyoming,
              are losing happiness quickly.

This is so sad, they say,
       the nobility is moving in,
              lords all over cow country.

Parents Furious After Schools
Are Forced to Cut Teachers

    Blood on the classroom floor
is bad education, says mom,
      poor pedagogy, adds dad.

How is this any better
    than Goth kids
shooting up the school cafeteria?

School
Cuts to
Go Ahead

      The school board
isn't about to listen
         to furious parents.

The knives come out
         tomorrow. The teachers, one hopes,
have a good hospital plan.

Tories Plan to Protect Same-Sex Opponents

If you're planning
    to oppose your woman
and you're a guy

    you're on your own.
Let the Liberals
    look after you.

Matches Made in Heaven

    In the other place
everyone has a light,
        and they're smoking all the time.

    The questions I have are:
who's working in the match
        factories up there?

    And do they have
fair labour practices in Paradise?

Trio Marches down the Niagara River to the Beat of Their Own Drum

    I hope they hang on
tight, and I hope that drum
      is big enough for three.

    In any trio
two of them will be same-sex
      drummers. I hope

they're on friendly terms,
      because the Tories
can't do anything about the Falls.

U.S. Diplomat Says
Passports Won't Hurt

    They will come with
blunt edges. There'll be no
        blood on the customs house floor.

You'll be allowed
        to carry them on board
past watchful security agents.

Gilliland
Captures
First Pole

    The pole was
immobile and standing
       straight up at the time.

David Gilliland stood
      with his arms around it,
breathing normally.

Two Paralyzed After Drinking Recalled Toxic Carrot Juice

It didn't taste funny at all,
said one victim, but I do remember
how flavourful it was.

I seem to see in my mind's eye
an unnatural orange hue,
put in his unfortunate partner.

Axe May Fall on Outdoor Centres

It has been hanging
    by the merest thread,
        or so it seems,

reports an apprehensive
    park board member
        on his way indoors.

The Secret Behind He Who Will End Secret Deals

It has certainly been a secret
      to I, who will wait
for the plain truth to emerge.

Us need to know
      what our government is
doing for we.

Car Air Purifier Smells Like Heaven

Presumably one's automobile
will be filled
with the scent of matches,

no matter the claims by
Platonists that the supernatural
doesn't appeal to the human senses at all.

Nightclub Owner Charged After Blood Mopped Up

Mickey Podheretz told this reporter
that the group of schoolteachers
was dripping blood when they
entered the premises.

Those were school cuts,
said the burly Podheretz,
not anything that happened
in my place.

I run a clean club here.
I don't know why they're
charging I.

Pilfering Patrons a Problem for Restaurants

We don't want to tie them to their chairs,
said restaurateur Malvolio Podborski,
but if people keep stealing our customers

I don't know what else to do.
It's especially irksome when they lift them
just before they pay their checks.

Teacher Remembered Different Ways

Educator Mervin Podnarchuck, who recently bled to death,
was famous around John Oliver Secondary School
for recalling streets no one else knew about.

Though his students might ride to school
along Broadway or Kingsway,
their mentor regaled them with tales
of his adventures on Straitway,
recommended by St. Paul,
and Beggarsway, a route used
during his childhood in Minneapolis.

Far-away places, with strange-sounding names,
he would sing, and his charges would
hum along with him.

Tories Pushed Over Leaky Condos

First I was puzzled
    by these buildings
        lying on their sides
            athwart the street.

When told of the Conservative action
    I immediately wondered
        why they would think
            that would improve anything.

Known Sex Offender Arrested and Charged with Sexual Assault on Transit Bus

As long as he restricted his attacks
to human beings of either sex
the authorities would only
keep tabs on him.

But when he targeted
the public conveyances
even they had to sing,
it was such an unnatural thing.

Mountie Probed in Sex Assault Case

A taste, said the presiding magistrate,
    of your own medicine.

At least, pleaded the policeman's counsellor,
    clear the courtroom.

As to the public conveyances, said the Crown,
    one is discouraged
        from entering by the rear door.

Why Woman was Left in Hospital Hallway to be Probed

It can now be revealed
    that a network of circumstances
        led to the unusual location.

All of our probing rooms
    were in use that afternoon,
        said head nurse Michelle Pordnicki,

and the patient insisted
    that the probe be performed
        as early as possible.

Besides which, our probational students
    were of such numbers
        that only the hallway would accommodate them.

Rumsfeld's Leadership "Inspired by God"

U.S. Defense Secretary Donald Rumsfeld,
according to General Peter Pace,
chairman of the Joint Chiefs of Staff,
swears that God told him
to kill as many of those people
  with unchristian names
  or none at all
  as fast as you can.

You know what they did in Baghdad
many years ago? They invented
reading and writing.

The president and the deity
and the defense secretary?
They know that if people get to
reading and writing,
      it's game over.

Arrival of New Treatments Have Hurt Firm

Many junior partners has left for other jobs.
The Chief Executive Officer are in tears.
Stocks is down. Confidence are gone.
A weeks of strong measure are indicated.
Communication are of prime importances
      until we gets this sorted out,
      but till then, we has to
      stop the bleeding, say
      company spokeman Morris Podnarski.

Following the Oyster Trail in Tofino

Those migrating mollusks,
heavy with a summer's ocean floor grazing,
light out for open seas
      every year about this time.

Oyster-lovers in the know
catch sight of that worn path in the sand
and, aw shucks, it's like taking candy
      in a barrel.

Seven Group Helps Iron Out Glitches in Digital Production

After untold aeons of five digits per hand and foot,
a bold experiment in finger production

prepares humankind for the complex future.

A dispute remains regarding the usefulness
of two additional toes,

and another about the necessity of
seven fingers for such simple tasks as ironing.

Religious Leaders Descend on Parliament Hill

Lay persons climbing the same hill
were astonished to see priests and imams,
TV evangelists and rabbis, zen roshi
and Dene medicine men

floating downward in a kind of reverse Ascension,
or being lowered from helicopters,
and one sky pilot hanging from his parachute.

Well, said an atheist halfway up the Hill,
it's better than axes falling on outdoor centres.

17-Year-Old Turns Himself Into Police

One has to applaud
such a nifty bit of legerdemain
at such a tender age.

But really? He
must look old and cynical
for his years.

Every Woman Counts, Governor-General Says

Hear that?: One, two, three, four, five, six,
              seven, eight, nine, ten male premiers
              in this country.

Hear that?: One female prime minister in
              one hundred and thirty-three years.

Hear that?: Knit two, purl one, knit
              two, purl one ....

Pregnant Cross Sightseeing on Granville Island

Now I've seen everything,
said Milo Padzinsky of Everett, Washington.

I mean the alpha and the omega
right here in the marketplace.

There is no word on when
we might expect the Blessed Event.

Thomson Learning to be Sold

It's hard to get the knack of it,
said Ontario's most famous painter.

When some stranger says name your price,
I always say Vincent.

He's a great collector, I replied,
but you'd better get back to your selling class.

Gender-Bending Deer Surprises Hunter

Castlegar resident Ernie Poderoff
is no stranger to interspecies sex.

Occasionally he will even woo a male ruminant.
But he likes to insist on being the aggressor.

So he was shocked last Saturday morning
to be on the receiving end of a forest probe.

I'm bamber, not bambee, he told the *Sun*.

I Knew It Was Wrong: Teacher

John Oliver Secondary School English instructor Murphy Pagnano
recently defended himself against a charge
of uttering dozens of dangling modifiers in his classroom.

Seeming to fall from the sky, he averred,
I could not escape the misplaced participle.

Salmon Pivotal in Defining Future of B.C. Native Relations

In a modern twist
on the old spin-the-bottle game,
British Columbia First Nations
and Provincial fisheries officials
found a new use
for smoked sockeye this weekend.

Valley

November

My humble offering to Lorine Niedecker

Cactus
   sage
        'n snake
where I walked
    my vally

a cowboy movie
to move through
as if a life
were myself on screen
being watched

or a Max Brand
novel, filled with
unlikelihood in cactus.

This way somehow
a secret from the parental ordinary,

*yet learning to be
in their valley —
              how to watch
the ground for snakes
     in cactus spines*

or the beautiful
spear grass, perfect
    miniature lances
in your socks.
        all literature

*at your fingertips
yanking porcupine quills
  from the dog's palate —
those lovely discards
  lying in the sun*

that simply shone
every day
is no one
I knew wore a shirt
save for school

*or in a restaurant
if he was
    a rich kid.*

a shirt in peach season I wore

> not to itch
>   in those trees —
>   no jazz in my sweat
> but juice in our kitchen
>   on my chest.

Peach trees
across a dirt road
    from sagebrush —
made a green
   line through the light brown.

So much water
in our desert, river
in lakes, irrigation
ditch, everything
filled with green

slime, long
    strands, heavy
on your face, so happily
        under water —
a map of the ancient

glacier. Lines
   on the rock face
a story too, a coyote
   tells us his lies
      as we listen

after dark.
   A howl echoes
off the bluff, music
   for a tricky heart,
mystery for a book boy.

Shelley could steer
as he read.

                This coyote boy
sat in a hillside cave,
    a western novel

in his left hand —
    God's brown grass
out in the sun,
    also his own land
        you are allowed.

Odor of sage
is memory, a purple
    refusal to rime
           ~~rave~~
with itself.

One's automobile
  will be filled
    with the scent of sage—
how wise to drive
  my valley

south. We Thought south
                our direction,
~~sun~~ leaning in
                from our south
on our ~~southern~~ side

where the light's foot beckons
& the brightness
begins.
But still
we'd watch the ground

>   before us—
>   listen for rattle
> of a fast tail,
>   head down
> as if humble.

My father
glistening with
perspiration
rounded Third &
otherwise

*carried lumber at work.
He taught me
to sweat, a five-mile
paper route,
 cleaning green slime*

from the empty town pool —
 sunstroke hospital, setting pins
with no shirt,
 okay in a small
town, lied about my age

to sweat in Mac 'n' Fitz
    packing house,
toiled in orchards,
    no Eden
in This valley,   tourists

loll on beaches
    or gobble cherries,
wonder where the air
    conditioning is, if they're
Americans.

Both my parents
    were born in Alberta,
came to The Okanagan
    as kids, The earth
        now semi-vertical.

The earth
    once under a glacier,
  so much made of rocks—
  round as apples,
    a dry round place

> where a coyote
>   sits 'n grins at me.
>   He wins
> every race we enter,
>   he's pointy face

*I'd call my little broTher
if he'd pay attention —
If he'd list me as oTher
under The striations
of This valley.*

There Then

December

Aarhus 1995

Every day I got lost
or lost my bearings
until I walked
past my loud friendly ducks.

Walked and walked
to where the Vikings
made a half-circle
to their liking, further

to the reconstituted bog
in which the red-haired
bog man lies, innocent
of all charges, long

as history. The Vikings
made a semi-circle
facing the sea,
from which my hiking
brought me
to this desiccate sleep.

Athens
Anaheim
Amsterdam

Berlin 1985

On that borrowed black and white set
West Berlin TV displayed a model
who took her clothes off.

East Berlin TV showed you how
to change your tires to conserve energy.

I went to the Ku'Damm
and ate my first German restaurant food,
a Hawaiian ham steak.

                    It was
forty years before that night that Adolf Hitler
shot himself.

Boston
Bergen
Buffalo

Calgary 1964

Proudly innocent, Biblical, twenty
something, I lectured foothills bigots
in letters to newspapers, opposed
the know-nothing ladies' organizations
from smaller towns, learned to live
below zero for weeks, reading books
they'd never dream of, corresponding
with San Francisco poets, over-
estimating my own strophes, a
corduroy bohemian with an eleven inch
TV. How far I felt from those
streets, how distant from their time,
how vertical I tried to be on their
wind-scraped surface!

Christchurch
Cuernavaca
Cape Town

Chicago 2001

Nobody could tell us
where the Red Line El stop was
but we found it and got on
and looked at the rain outside.

I moped and complained, no
baseball for me, no Wrigley
dream, but we persisted, what
else could we do, and so
did 30,000 others who
understood their way. We insisted

on the centre field bleachers,
sat with motorcycle dudes drinking
mai-tais under a 90 degrees
overcast, happy in Cubs town,
I sat purring beside my girl

down in Illinois, imagine, mai-
tais in Chi, imagine, it's
as if a person might win
in late innings.

Chelsea
Chase
Chihuahua

Dubrovnik 1966

       Skeletal Romans stand in underwater valleys,
       blue Adriatic mountain top islands
       elude all politics, all conquerors.
       There's a swimsuit in my pack, I think.

The hillsides are full of bullets, but yellow broom
shines below the cypresses, scents our open windows;
road signs sprout Cyrillic words, then here's

       one palm tree,
       one orthodox dome,
       one Dubrovnik,
       one drawbridge,
       no automobiles, no scooters, no bikes,
       maybe some Shakespeare.

And on Mt. Sergio looking down, the thin fierce
Montenegro people, hawks, standing high,
straight noses, high cheekbones, black hair, piercing black eyes.
Innocent and deadly, ancient and quiet.

                                       Detroit
                                       Düsseldorf
                                       Dallas

Edmonton 2001

My daughter lives in Edmonton!
I left her there a few years back
and now I write iambic verse
or prose that ambles in its track.

My daughter's cold in Edmonton.
She lives a life I do not know.
I used to live in Calgary
and co-existed with the snow.

Alberta isn't where we live.
Iambic isn't what I write.
Why doesn't she come back to town?
Why do I have to get this right?

My daughter's there in Edmonton
where pick-up trucks are what they drive.
I hope free verse comes back to me,
and so does she while I'm alive.

Everett
Edirne
Eugene

Ft. Smith 1975

White pelicans
wading in the rapids
of the Slave,

didn't I see you
in Veracruz?

Didn't I tell you
it was safe
up here?

Florence
Fargo
Fasano

Greenwood 1942

Shortly after I burned the hillside down
I fell in love with the ranger's daughter
who had comic books. I had no
comic books. Her father's job involved
trees on fire. So did my father's,
or at least smoke as watched
through magnifying lenses. I sat in our
tent and read her comic books while
my father hiked down for groceries. Outside
the tent an animal snuffled. In the morning
my father was there and we had porridge
again. I was not fully aware of myself
but I went step by step on that
mountain top, helping my father watch out
for anyone burning any of the others.

Guatemala
Grand Forks
Gorizia

Helsinki 1995

At 1:25 a.m.
      in front of the Grand Marina Hotel
they were still doing a loud sound check
      for the band. Oh boy,
the sun would just not go down,
      but beer would, vodka would,
drunken teenagers will spill it on you,
      till you step over some sleeping ones,
head for bed, read a book
      with no light on, listen
to these icemen doing their midsummer
      sound check, while the odor of
barbecued herring seeps into
      your dreams.

Halifax
Honolulu
Havre

Indianapolis 1998

In the centre of the USA
is Indiana.
In the centre of Indiana
is Indianapolis.
In the centre of Indianapolis
is Monument Circle.
In the centre of Monument Circle
is the State Soldiers' and Sailors' Monument.

It's a tall needle made by Germans
in 1901, to celebrate USAmerican war victories till then.
One of the wars it celebrates
is victory over the Indians.

Looking around, I didn't see any
Indian people in their polis.
And I thought: if anyone had raised
this kind of monument in, say, Winnipeg,
the Indian people would have
pulled it down like golden boys.

Istanbul
Irapuato
Inuvik

Juárez 1964

There was no form
       in the middle of the bridge,
only the news
       that we were leaving fear behind.

In El Paso the night before
       I tried not to imagine
a bullet in my back. In the morning
       we saw tall men in suits and ties

walking nervously by short poor
       Mexicanos standing on rubber soles.
Now across the bridge
       I am that he whose brains
       are scattered
            aimlessly

not looking for a form
       but listening to music
       and hoping to recall it.

Jasper
Johannesburg
Joliette

Krakow 2001

After all these years, I'm
    walking a dog on a leash again,
sniffing our way
    down Grodska, an old Dachshund
and a widower, white
    whiskers on both.

"Hello, Raban," say old women we meet,
    "Dzien dobry, Raban," intone couples.
And Raban, he knows
    every blade of grass
that forces its way
    through old pre-socialist concrete,
every dusty blade of grass
    and every dog that has visited.

Köln
Kamloops
Kavala

London 1990

On the Picadilly tube
above ground from Heathrow, he
held a suitcase and shoulder bag in front of him,
held a—came one half-inch
from throwing up in the crowd.

A half pint of bitter
in the Sail and Bower,
sixties music cutting through cigarette smoke
made him better;
spaghetti puttenesca
made him Roman.

Nearly puked—happens at times.
He knew what goes into a stomach
and what should. A bag of crisps
out of a machine—20p.

Lisbon
Los Angeles
Limón

México 1964

Four of us, movie stars
    sat in the sun at Plaza de México,
biggest ring in the world
    to watch the *novilleros*—

it was spotty, dangerous, rather dull.
    But the first guy was gored
on his first pass with his first bull,
    and the other two had to do
    the business of seven animals.

One guy got gored three times, ah
    novilleros! There was one
good *picador*, an old fat white haired guy
    with a very good white horse,
    mattress on its side.

And one big laugh, a *banderillero*'s
    pink-clad ass running for safety.
There was much discontent
    and fighting in the crowd.
And no Nobel prize holders.

Melbourne
Montréal
Minneapolis

New York 1989

Lots of famous New Year death, maybe
too much. The Ceausescus
executed against a wall, someone
who recently got the Order of Canada
died in Québec City, Samuel Beckett
died on Friday like you know who,
Doug Harvey died of liver, but
the *New York Times* was moved
by the death of Billy Martin, killed
because he wouldn't wear a seat belt.

Thea and I had a look at
St. Patrick's Cathedral, surrounded by
police wooden horses, for Billy's
funeral. Call it crap's last jape.

New Orleans
Nuremberg
Niagara Falls

Oaxaca 1965

Ancient deserted cities
    Monte Albán and Mitla
with Oaxaca between
    spells mom,
        but here
beautiful boys play café guitar,
sell Chiclets,
    guide *gringos,*

kids alone in the square, not
    a *madre* in sight,

just a church the fathers
    papered with gold
        that *Indios*

were allowed to touch—
        once.

Ottawa
Oslo
Oklahoma City

Port Colborne 2003

I saw the whole town
    from a rented wheelchair.
My love set me down
    by the famous canal.
She wheeled me around
    and parked me on sidewalks.
I felt like a clown
    with a nimble director.
I lost my renown
    but gained me a girlfriend.
She didn't once frown
    though I yelled like an idiot.

When I could walk
    she stood by to catch me.
I love her, I love her,
    I told her I love her.

Perth
Papeete
Plovdiv

Phoenix 2004

The bar is full of cigarette smoke
but the air outside is dry as my childhood.
They can carry handguns into the bar
but look, there's a bead shop, Jean.
It's only USAmerican beer in the bar
but anapests go with cactuses, huh?
The wide sky is filled with jet fighters
but here's the most important news:
it's March fifteenth and we're watching
the Giants and the Cubs
and we're not wearing jackets
and we haven't been shot at yet.

Philippopolis
Phelps
Philipsburg

Québec 1954

A buzz through his body
of envy he felt
as he stood on the edge
of the actual field

of history.
        He stept beside another real,
this western teenager, out
        of the anapest
        or nearly.

        Down to the old city
looking for a Champlain stone
        to touch,
        to seal
somehow the strange years
he could see
        and tell no one about.

Qu'Appelle
Queretero
Qualicum

Rome 1985, 1996, 2006

Once a decade I
get into the Holy See queue,
I marvel at the twisted columns,
shuffle past the expired Papas,
creep down the halls of hammered antiquities,
climb stairs, try not to annoy strangers,
anticipate Michael Angelo,
and finally! squeeze into the Sistine Chapel.

It is worth it, the long plane flight,
the long walk through Eternal town,
the slow snake of tourists,
to stand here, to catch glimpses
of this venerable black and white floor.

Rivière-du-Loup
Reading
Reims

San José 1978

I sat in the park to watch
the Ticos pass on Avenida Centrál.
The prostitutes signified by smoking cigarettes,
as Latinas think only a whore would
smoke on the street. This one wasn't even
a smoker. She tossed away her Derby
and started on me.
                        She sat beside me
and asked whether I were German. No,
I said one more time. She asked whether
I were married. Darn tootin', I said
in Spanish. She took a fly out of my hair
and managed to touch me several times,
I wasn't counting.
                      I must have been such
a disappointment. In Guatemala the big-eyed
boy tried to get me to a Turkish bath.
In Florence the U.S. professors loitered
around Donatello's David.
                      Everyone
fails to fuck me. In San José
I was a long way from any rich coast.

Sofia
St. Louis
Sydney

Sheridan 1968

It was one of their patriotic holidays,
Veterans Day or July the Fourth
or Decoration Day or Armed Forces Day
or Memorial Day or Flag Day,
one of those remember the Alamo,
remember the Maine, remember Pearl Harbor,
remember Little Big Horn, remember
the Gulf of Tonkin days.
      The town
was shut down and dusty and hot, and we
just wanted a salad and ginger ale,
so we parked and perambulated
the sidewalk.
     There, in a store front
we saw one terrific holiday display:
red white and blue ribbons, then
nothing at all, but in the middle
of a white tablecloth, a solitary
hand grenade.

Sherbrooke
Shelburne
Shakespeare

Trieste 1977

At the ruins
 of the Roman theatre
behind the police station
 a thin old woman
feeds spaghetti
 to a dozen skinny cats.

I am like them
 or her, it is
up to you to guess
 which.

Toledo
Toronto
Tucson

Thessaloniki 1966

When St. Paul of Tarsus came here
did they serve him fish he didn't recognize?
Did the dust fly like traffic
through the city, around bodies
that desired to be elsewhere?
Did the workers in the bank pass
his paper from desk to desk,
stamping and stapling, frowning and shouting?
Did St. Paul of Tarsus
dream of a machine gun,
invoke the name of his Lord,
gather up his travelling clothes
and turn his face south, giving up
these townsfolk never to be saved?

Thorold
Thunder Bay
Thatcham

Union Bay 1964

When the sun
    as it sometimes does
lies along the coast
    the heap of oyster shells
goes bright
    white
beside the rain-weathered
    café, something I love
to see, but not
    eat.

Union Gap
Utica
Udine

Verona 1966

Except for Tony Bellette,
I was the only gentleman I knew in Verona,
and not much of one, to tell the truth,
which I always do in poems, as McFadden would say,
until I found Dante Alighieri
in the middle of a clear plaza
and all the other poets on rooftops
looking down toward him
and for the moment
me.

Vera Cruz
Vyborg
Vienna

Wellington 1984

A tree with small lemons
on a hilltop above Katherine Mansfield
did not hide the sun.
The sun was in the north
and I was in the south
looking for a sour story.
Down the hill road just a little
from Tony Bellette's house
was a fish and chip shack
with malt vinegar.
We listened while
the tones led us down and up again.

Winnipeg
Windsor
Williams Lake

White Rock 1942

The car slides on ice
and your heart is sick with fear.
The little campfire gets away
and you can't stop its rise.
The tide is coming in fast
and you aren't familiar with tides
and now you are on a sand island
and need to run and swim or die
in a place you've never seen before,
water salty and moving
and full of teeth
or deep pulling holes.

Whitehorse
Wheeling
Whitby

Xalapa 1964

All the houses
are reached by climbing hills
down which spill
flowers on branches
reaching out of these
wispy clouds, and high
above all those giant black round
Asian African heads
carved in basalt
no one in Xalapa
has ever seen
elsewhere in this world.
                              It is
one of those legendary cities
you soon cease
to ask questions about, but only
fall down one or all of those hills
in the prose you
brought with you.

Xochimilco
Xeres de la Frontera
Xcaret

York 1990

With my blind and best
    friend Willy
I walked the renowned
    wall. Then we stood
in Christ's place
    on the cross
on the old sad floor
    of the Minster
and he turned on his little
    recorder to catch his
photo of the trip, the unseen
    virgin men singing ancient
Christian song. In my best
    friend's family county
and I thinking of Toledo.
    I didn't die there
either.

Yuma
Ypsilanti
Yellowknife

Zürich 1995

Here at the end of my travels
I can't get into the city;
I'm forever at the airport,
at the train station,
looking for Hilda D. up the lake.

I can't ever get downtown
where the self-satisfied bankers
do not await me. I know
women here, but will never
see them. I want to take a bus
to a café near the cathedral
and order *raclette* on a blue plate.

But I'll always be here at the edge,
almost not anywhere, nearly
asleep, tired of letters
and unable to speak the language.

Zacatecas
Zadar
Zenith